the
Shaman's
Quest

the Shaman's Quest

Journeys in an Ancient Spiritual Practice

Nevill Drury

With a Basic Introduction to Shamanism by Tom Cowan

Walking Together, Finding the Way
SKYLIGHT PATHS Publishing
Woodstock, Vermont

The Shaman's Quest:
Journeys in an Ancient Spiritual Practice

2002 First SkyLight Paths Edition
© 2001 by Nevill Drury
Introduction © 2002 by Tom Cowan

Library of Congress Cataloging-in-Publication Data
Drury, Nevill, 1947–
The shaman's quest : journeys in an ancient spiritual practice / Nevill Drury ;
with an introduction to shamanism by Tom Cowan. — 1st SkyLight Paths ed.
        p. cm.
ISBN 1-893361-68-3
1. Shamanism. I. Title.
BL2370.S5 D784 2002
291.1'44—dc21

                                                                    2002010253

10 9 8 7 6 5 4 3 2 1

Manufactured in the United States of America

SkyLight Paths Publishing is creating a place where people of
different spiritual traditions come together for challenge and
inspiration, a place where we can help each other understand the
mystery that lies at the heart of our existence.

SkyLight Paths sees both believers and seekers as a community that
increasingly transcends traditional boundaries of religion and
denomination—people wanting to learn from each other, *walking
together, finding the way.*

SkyLight Paths, "Walking Together, Finding the Way" and colophon are
trademarks of LongHill Partners, Inc., registered in the U.S. Patent and
Trademark Office.

Published by SkyLight Paths Publishing
A Division of LongHill Partners, Inc.
Sunset Farm Offices, Route 4, P.O. Box 237
Woodstock, VT 05091
Tel: (802) 457-4000 Fax: (802) 457-4004
www.skylightpaths.com

CONTENTS

*And the Great Spirit sent forth a sacred song
which could be heard in all corners of the world,
and shamans were summoned forth—
from North, South, East and West*

*And then these shamans journeyed to the
center of the world, so they could serve as
witnesses to the healing of the Earth*

A BASIC
INTRODUCTION TO
SHAMANISM

When the Earth speaks, shamans listen.

When the planet cries out in distress, shamans respond.

It has always been so.

In *The Shaman's Quest* Nevill Drury reminds us that the Call of the Earth transcends language, culture, ethnicity, time, distance, and location. For the shaman's world—our world—is one; and no matter where shamans live and practice they share a common ground of understanding and wisdom. Although they may reside in different quarters of the globe, they live in the same landscape of spirit and power.

In *The Shaman's Quest* we meet four shamans from four very different indigenous cultures, but each culture is still imbued with the ancient mysteries that call the shaman to lead an extraordinary life. Enoyuk rides his drum through the Arctic nights to comb the hair of a sea goddess beneath the frozen water; Kalu strides along the Songlines of his ancient creator-ancestors in the Australian outback; Saimei flies through the trees of Japan with her kami-spirits; and Baiya, deep in the South American rain forest, meets the powerful serpent spirits through the Mother Yajé plant. Here are four varieties of shamanic experience, which collectively reveal the essential core features of the shaman's life wherever he or she may live.

For perhaps forty thousand years, or even longer—no one really knows—human cultures have produced men and women whom today we refer to as "shamans." Historically, Shamanism first emerged in hunting-gathering communities, and today it survives most successfully in those modern indigenous communities that still retain a strong Earth-based way of life. Throughout the centuries shamans have provided essential services for their people. The work of the shaman is a human response to human problems and situations. From origins now lost in the prehistoric past, Shamanism continues to satisfy human needs today, or it would have died out long ago. Shamanism survives because it works, even in our highly techno-logized world that seems so far away from the tribal, village communities of our ancestors.

We are still human souls trying to live with the Soul of the Earth in ways that promote health and well-being for both. When the Earth suffers, we suffer; when the Earth is healthy, we are healthy. Knowing this, shamans become intermediaries between the human community and the great diversity of life that makes up this marvelous planet on which we live.

Each of the shamans in Drury's tales embarks on three quests to realize this role.

The first quest is the initiatory call to become a shaman. The second is the lifelong quest to restore health and power to their people and the land where they live. The third quest, as told here in the language of myth and mystery, is a more cosmic quest to answer a haunting call from the most ancient of spirits residing in a Sacred Lake that Drury calls the place where "All Things Come Forth." This is the call to restore order and balance to the Whole, an apocalyptic quest on which hangs the fate of Earth itself. In this quest, we the readers hear the urgency that faces each of us every day to save the planet on which we live.

The shaman speaks a language of myth and symbol— the language of stories—and it is in stories that Nevill Drury skillfully introduces us to the essential features of "core Shamanism."

Core Shamanism refers to the complex of visionary and healing techniques that are nearly universal and found in almost all shamanic cultures. We might think of them as the shaman's repertoire of spiritual and healing practices that transcend any specific culture and are successfully utilized by serious shamanic practitioners the world over. The term was introduced over thirty years ago by the renowned anthropologist, teacher, and shaman Michael Harner. Today it is a respected and well-validated mode of healing. The same core principles and practices that Drury's four shamans embody in their respective and exotic cultures are now currently established in many places around the world through the work of Harner-trained shamanic practitioners and indigenously trained shamans from native communities. In some places the two types of shamans work and train together, supporting each other's commitment to healing Earth and its inhabitants.

Core Shamanism has played a major role in the worldwide revival of Shamanism, seen in some of the most disparate places. For example, Shamanism has received official recognition from the government of the Republic of Tuva in central Asia, where the word *shaman* originated and where Western practitioners of core Shamanism were honored as shamanic healers by indigenous Tuvan shamans. On this side of the globe, a health maintenance organization plan in Madison, Wisconsin, has recently added coverage for shamanic counseling and healing work. In my own shamanic work I have been privileged to know practitioners who use core Shamanism in the most diverse settings: in the corporate world to restore the souls of individual employees and the corporation itself; among street gangs in inner cities to give youths-at-risk a sense of personal pride to replace violent, ego-driven behavior; among elementary school children to teach them the ways that Native Americans honored and respected the land and animals; and even at meetings of a White House environmental commission to bring a spirit of cooperation and harmony to rancorous discussions and arguments. Indeed, Shamanism continues to meet the human needs of vastly diversified communities. When the call for healing arises, shamans answer.

What are the core features of Shamanism? What makes someone a shaman?

The shaman is a man or woman who hears a call to be a special type of healer in his or her community. Often the call comes while the young man or woman is undergoing a severe illness or near-death experience. Such a traumatic event can loosen the hold that ordinary reality has over human consciousness, replacing it with a vision of a different, non-ordinary reality.

The concept of ordinary and non-ordinary realities is crucial to understanding shamanic work. Everyone experiences different types of reality: in dreams, reveries, intoxicated states, exhaustion, intense concentration at work or play, and sheer delight, to name only a few. Each of these suggests that there is some "otherworld" of experience that is accessible to us, but only under certain conditions. The shaman is an expert in creating those conditions that allow visionary experiences to emerge so that he or she can move into those non-ordinary realms to gain knowledge, understanding, wisdom, and healing power for the community.

Shamans worldwide share similar views of the cosmos that distinguish specific regions of non-ordinary reality, collectively called the Otherworld. One of these is a realm lying below the surface of the physical world, a kind of Lower or Under World, entered through caves, crevices, tree roots, springs, wells, the sea. Correspondingly, there is a region lying just beyond the sky, an Upper World reached by soul flights through the clouds, rainbows, sunbeams, or star tracks. And indeed there are portals right here in the physical Middle World—mists, fog, quirky turns in the road, "thin places" lurking on the other side of a tree or between two unusual stones—that allow the shaman to slip into a non-ordinary, spiritual dimension of the natural world itself. And so, from a familiar place in the ordinary world, the shaman finds doorways and entrances that lead deep below the surface of the Earth, high beyond the farthest stars, or into a timeless warp just around the next corner. In these four stories you will journey with shamans as they explore these realms and bring back power for their people.

From journeys into the spirit world, the apprentice shaman learns many things, both from the spirits themselves and from elder shamans who help the novices understand and interpret their visions. On their journeys, shamans discover ways to harness the spiritual energy in physical objects—such as stones, bones, feathers, drums, rattles, and sacred plants—to restore health to the sick and dispirited. In the eyes of the community, the apprentice shaman becomes a special person. People watch closely to see if the novice does indeed have healing skills to successfully perform the shaman's traditional tasks.

The core responsibilities of shamans are: to remove from someone the harmful energies that cause sickness and despair; to retrieve lost or stolen souls and restore health to the ill or dying; to interpret dreams, omens, and messages from the spirit world; to conduct rites of passage that prepare people for the next stages of their lives; to assist at births, receiving the human soul into this world; and to officiate at deaths by escorting the soul back into the Otherworld from which it came. It is only by witnessing successful, practical results in these areas that a community will honor a man or woman as a shaman. Should shamans lose the ability to do healing work—often spoken of as the shamans' helping spirits leaving them—then they are no longer recognized as shamans.

In addition to healing individuals, shamans play an essential role in reminding their people of the sacredness of human life. In indigenous cultures every aspect of life was considered sacred, a reflection of mythic actions first performed eons ago by the ancestors, often thought of as supernatural, almost godlike beings. The "original instructions" seen in their lives created templates for future generations to know how to live with one another and the Earth itself. When humans forget these instructions or carelessly disregard them, disasters result. Crops fail, the hunts are unsuccessful, food becomes scarce, proper weather does not arrive in its appropriate season, children are unhealthy and die young, the old become dispirited, war erupts, people live in fear.

In meeting human and environmental catastrophes such as these, the shaman embodies a long-held belief among tribal people that human life on Earth must be conducted in harmony with greater powers, with the spirits and deities of nature and the universe, and with the will of the Creator. Only then will peace, love, and harmony flourish.

This concept of living in harmony with the universe is found the world over. Most indigenous cultures have a special term or word for this harmonious state and encourage their peoples to live in accordance with it. Everyone is expected to respect both the natural and supernatural worlds to keep those worlds in balance. But it is the shaman's duty to maintain that balance when individuals disrupt it through carelessness, wickedness, or ignorance. Then the shaman steps in to cleanse and renew the community through ritual and healing ceremonies, and recreate the original harmony between our mortal world and the world of the spirits.

The shaman stays in touch with the beauty, music, and harmony of the cosmos, what the Celtic traditions refer to as the Great Song, the *Oran Mór*. This is the music that is always playing, sometimes heard in the faery music that leads mortals into otherworldly realms, the music of heaven, the choirs of angels, the whispering of the ancestors, the songs of the birds, the voices in the wind, the melodies of the mountain stream falling over rocks. Indeed, the stones themselves are singing whether or not we hear, whether or not we even listen.

In the four stories that follow, each shaman hears and responds to this music which Drury richly describes as "a glorious and wonderful song...the Song of the Great Spirit...the sacred Song of Healing," which has "always existed, even before the creation of the world." Perhaps these shamans, and others like them, will indeed return from the Sacred Lake of Spirit bringing a message of peace and healing. Perhaps we, and others, will hear it. And perhaps the Great Song will find new life in our hearts and souls; and once again we and the Earth will live and sing in harmony and hope.

THE SHAMAN'S QUEST

NORTH

As dawn washed pink-grey shadows across the icy foreshore, Enoyuk looked out from the entrance of his snowhouse. On his lined and rugged face he felt a mild breeze sweeping in across the bay, from the direction of the headland known as Three Ravens. Here and there the wafting breeze lifted little flurries of snow, brushing across the rocky outcrops where Enoyuk and his people had built their winter camp.

It was certainly a better day today, and winter would soon be at an end. For a short time at least there would be a reprieve from the buffeting gales that had swept forcefully across the bay night after night, lashing the fishing boats and howling around the entrances to the snowhouses. In this season now passing, hunting near the edge of the ice floes had been hazardous indeed, the fierce winter swell pounding the jagged shores with large waves and treacherous currents. Only the very strongest and most skillful hunters could venture forth in seas like this.

For those hunting along the icy shoreline itself there were problems of a different kind. Seemingly firm, snow-covered formations could subside treacherously underfoot at any time. Fierce snow-storms could rise up without warning, and blind the hunter in his tracks—making each and every step increasingly perilous. Even in favorable conditions, when one could see a clear path ahead, great reserves of patience and calm were called for. At those special moments when the hunter could hear the huffing of a seal catching its breath beneath an ice hole, he would still have to maintain the strictest sense of silence—and then throw his harpoon suddenly, and with all his might, into the dark hole in the ice. If he was lucky he would strike his prey, and could then call upon his fellow hunters to help haul the heavy, slippery carcass onto the ice.

This year, the catches had been fewer, and the seals themselves much smaller than in seasons past. Enoyuk remembered times of great hunting when giant square-flipper seals were harpooned from kayaks and brought ashore, and a prized moment when he and his brothers had forced a whale into a shallow inlet, causing it to beach on the rocks. For many weeks afterward the families had feasted on whale meat, and on the fat beneath its hide—always considered a great delicacy. And in this time of abundance there had also been ample supplies of seal-fat for heating their snowhouses, cooking their meat and drying their dank clothes.

Now, though, times had changed. It seemed that Nuliajuk, Mistress of the Sea Animals, was no longer favorably disposed toward Enoyuk's camp. Perhaps some members of the group had done forbidden things in secret—for when one transgressed the sacred teachings, the curses unleashed by violating these laws would then float down beneath the waves and darken Nuliajuk's skin with a grimy coating that was hard for her to remove. Perhaps Tyara or

Udluriak had cooked caribou meat over ice instead of on dry land, as was the custom among his people? He wondered, too, whether Kadlajuk had harpooned a seal without seeking permission to take its flesh for food? Or whether Moraq had caused offense to the animal-spirits by calling his prey by their secret, personal names instead of by their familiar hunting titles?

Certainly, if forbidden deeds like this had taken place, Nuliajuk would be greatly angered and her rage would bring much harm upon the camp. For it was well known that she had a special pool at the bottom of the ocean where she kept her seals and whales and walruses, and when sacred laws were broken she would keep back her sea animals and not release them for the hunt. At those times it would fall to Enoyuk himself to appease her, for he alone was the shaman-healer of his camp. He alone could make the spirit-journey beneath the waves, traveling fearlessly to Nuliajuk's stone fortress at the bottom of the ocean, in order to make amends for the misdeeds of his people. He alone could take Nuliajuk's comb in his hands and gently untangle her matted hair, while scraping the grime of wrongdoings from her body. He alone knew special spirit-songs of the deep which he could sing to her, urging her to forgive the transgressions which had taken place. He alone could urge her to command the creatures of her domain to once again go forth into the sea, yielding their flesh as food and spirit-sustenance for the group.

Enoyuk reflected on the tales that he had learned about the great Goddess of the Sea when he was still only a child. His grandmother Kinalik, who always enchanted him with her stories of the spirits and the ancient ways, had told him around the campfire at night how Nuliajuk was once a beautiful young woman, with many admirers who sought her hand in marriage. Not finding any of them to her liking, she went far away from her camp and lived for a time by herself. After this period of seclusion she took a bird husband—a petrel or "bird of the storm"—who promised her a life of leisure and luxury and took her away to live on an island. However, the bird-husband's promises of a pleasureable lifestyle soon proved empty and misleading and Nuliajuk became saddened and distraught by this cruel twist of fate. She now called for her father to rescue her, and in response he came swiftly to the island and killed the bird-husband who had trapped and misled her there. But as the father and daughter sought to escape from the island in their small boat, friends of the dead petrel summoned a fierce storm which threatened to capsize them both amidst mountainous seas.

Thinking now only of his own safety, and keen to lighten his load, Nuliajuk's father threw his daughter overboard and in desperation she was forced to cling tightly to the side of the boat. And yet his selfishness and cruelty knew no bounds for he now began to chop her fingers off one by one with his hunting knife, till at last she could hold on no longer and fell down into the depths of the ocean.

Mysteriously, she did not drown. Nuliajuk's severed fingers transformed into whales and seals and walruses, and Nuliajuk herself became the Great Goddess of the Sea, with mastery over all its creatures. As a Great Goddess she would retain her beauty forever but as a consequence of her father's cruelty she now had no fingers to hold a comb or braid her matted hair. Nevertheless, the sea animals had helped her build a stone fortress at the bottom of the sea, protected by large boulders and a fierce sea-dog guardian. As Enoyuk's grandmother explained, according to the wisdom teachings only the most powerful shaman within each hunting community was allowed to visit Nuliajuk's domain, and only when enticed by sacred songs would she consent to have the shaman comb her hair.

Enoyuk remembered, too, how he himself had become a shaman those long years past. In those early days, when he was still little more than a youth, he had had a vivid dream, and in this dream he was visited by the spirit of a polar bear—the Great White One—who seemed to shine in the dark and who told him he would one day become a great hunter and magician. Enoyuk told this dream to his father, and his father then took him to meet the wise and esteemed Alareak, who at that time was considered one of the greatest shamans among the northern peoples.

Alareak had built his snowhouse on a rocky crag at the edge of the camp—on an outcrop known as Eagle's Claw. Alareak lived only with his three aging husky dogs—survivors of the dog-team which had pulled his snow-sledge when he was more actively engaged with everyday hunting. His wife had long since departed for the spirit world and he had no children of his own to whom he could pass his sacred knowledge. Many in the community found his manner distant and aloof—but everyone honored and respected him.

For a while Alareak did not respond to the presence of the young man who now stood before him, and he appeared to engage in silence only with his own thoughts. But he then bade Enoyuk to enter his snowhouse and take his place upon the caribou skins strewn across the floor. Looking deeply into the recesses of his soul, he now told Enoyuk that the Great White One was a wise and powerful teacher and a great spirit-helper, and that it was indeed a good omen that he had come to visit in the dream. He also explained that to become a shaman was a great calling, and one that required considerable strength, patience and discipline—qualities that could only be earned through personal experience.

Alareak now engaged in an earnest discussion with Enoyuk's father, finally agreeing that he would tutor his son as a trainee shaman. He then accepted the gift of a tent pole embellished with the wing of a sea-gull—a sign to the master shaman that the young apprentice wished to learn how to fly in the spirit world.

Alareak now instructed Enoyuk to sit in silence on a snow sledge, far away from the community. For five days Enoyuk sat there on the sledge in the very depths of winter, desolate and very much alone, feeling that he had been abandoned and thinking that perhaps this was all a terrible mistake. At night strange and eerie animal-calls would fill the air and strong, icy winds would buffet him from all sides. And although he was clothed in a heavy fur-lined jacket and was wearing leather mittens and sealskin boots, an aching coldness still found its way into every limb of his body.

Finally Alareak came to see how he was coping and told him that he could now come to stay inside a small snowhouse which had been especially built for his initiation. Here he would have to sit silently on a small raised platform, again without food or drink, and cast his mind only upon the all-embracing power of the Great Spirit, and upon the task of summoning tunraqs, or magical allies. Alareak explained to Enoyuk that these helper spirits would appear to him in his visions at a time of *their* choosing—and *only* if he was considered worthy.

For five days Enoyuk sat in the freezing snow-house, contemplating the Great Spirit, summoning all the reserves of patience and endurance he could muster, and calling from within his soul for helper allies—as he had been instructed. While he felt more protected within the snowhouse than on the snow-sledge, he still felt miserable in his isolation and now was cramped and confined in a way he hadn't experienced before. On the sixth day Alareak appeared again, and this time offered a small drink of lukewarm water. Seven days later he came once more, this time with another drink of water and a small piece of meat. These would have to sustain Enoyuk on his vision-quest for a further ten days.

As days and nights flowed into each other in a pattern of desolate and unending repetition, Enoyuk felt his personal resolve sinking—and he began to descend into an intense abyss of alienation and despair. He seemed utterly forsaken, utterly without any sense of companionship or purpose. But then, quite suddenly, a dramatic change occurred. Without any expectation, and in a complete reversal of all that had gone before, he now discovered that he was no longer aware of the passage of time. He seemed at last to disengage from the pain of his ordeal, moving beyond icy fatigue and isolation into a realm sustained by an increasing sense of inner warmth. He now felt as if an altogether different world was nourishing and supporting him—a world of spirit, peace and calm far removed from the agonizing cycle of blisteringly cold days and storm-swept nights. And now the spirit-beings began to show themselves before him too—in darting flashes and quick movements to begin with, but then within waves of radiant, luminescent colors that were awesome to behold.

At first Enoyuk felt that perhaps he had journeyed right into the very heart of the Northern Lights whose beautiful glow illumined the heavens, providing—as his grandmother had often reminded him—a torch-lit pathway for the spirits of the dead. Now and then in the haze of moving colors he seemed to snatch a glimpse of the Old Ones—those of his ancestors who had passed into death many years before, but whose wisdom and insight still guided the ways of the living. Then, from amidst the vivid colors he saw a small white bird—a fluffy ptarmigan—which now presented itself before him, catching his attention with its dark, intense eyes. Opening its wings to reveal a small hunting knife, it spoke to him in words which seemed to come from within its very being: "Take this knife and plunge it into my breast with a single strike. Eat of my flesh. Be nourished by my spirit. Take my strength as an offering, for your first guardian upon the shaman's path will soon come before you. On this encounter you will need to be strong."

Enoyuk at first resisted, for he loved these gentle snow-birds and wished them no harm. But realizing that he had to follow these instructions he reached for the small knife and plunged it with a single action into the heart of the little bird. Peeling away its delicate white feathers he exposed its dark red flesh with the knife and began to take nourishment from its body, as he had been told.

Now he became aware of a much larger creature approaching, and all at once he felt the awesome presence of the Great White One close at hand. Never in all his hunting days, and not since his vivid dream, had Enoyuk come so close to a polar bear. Instantly, and without warning, he could see every bristle of its dense white fur, every tiny pore on its glistening nose, every hint of light in its dark brown eyes, every pointed tip of its sharp teeth. Frozen with fear, Enoyuk was sure that this was his last moment as a living being. But now, in a movement that took him completely by surprise, the Great White One placed its wet nose hard against Enoyuk's face and he could feel the warmth of its dank breath across his cheeks and in his nostrils. Then, just as he was recovering from the sheer shock of this encounter, suddenly it was Alareak's face that now confronted him—for in a sudden and magical transformation the head of the polar bear melted away, dissolving in an arc of soft light. Now it was Alareak who stood before him... with a broad grin on his bronze-tanned face!

For a while neither spoke. Time itself seemed suspended in that magical encounter. But then Alareak said simply: "You did well. You understood the lesson. You faced the Great White One and you shared breath together. And you restrained your fear." The two men then sat down beside each other without speaking. Shadows flickered across the wall of the snowhouse before Alareak finally broke the silence: "Wait here for me. I have to go away for a short time. We will continue tomorrow evening at Eagle's Claw, and I will drum for you."

In Alareak's larger and more welcoming snow-house, Enoyuk felt much more at ease. For this, after all, was the home of the great shaman, a place where the helper-spirits would also come when summoned. Alareak kept his special shaman-drum wrapped in a heavy woollen blanket and handled it reverently as he showed it for the first time to his young companion. "This drum will help you journey further than all the snow sledges and husky-dogs in the camp," he said quietly. "This drum will take you far upon your spirit-quest."

As Enoyuk looked down at the rim of the drum he could see different creatures painted along its edge. "Those are my spirits, my tunraqs," said Alareak. "Every shaman must have his own spirits, for everyone needs strong guardians on the journey. When I drum for you your soul will come forth from your body, but in the spirit-world the shaman needs to know where to go." He chuckled softly and then said teasingly to Enoyuk, "You might lose your body on these journeys, but your soul will never become lost if you have tunraqs to guide you on the path."

Toward evening on the following day Alareak returned and began to prepare for Enoyuk's soul-journey. Clearing space within the ice house, Alareak placed his small stone lamp in the center, poured in a small quantity of seal-oil, and then lit the thin strip of dried moss which served as a wick. Immediately shadows began to dance across the walls, exciting Enoyuk's imagination and filling him with eager anticipation. Alareak, meanwhile, reached for his shaman-drum and also brought out a time-worn rattle which, like the drum, was inscribed with motifs of his spirit-helpers.

"First I must call to the spirits to let them know we are beginning now," said Alareak. "Then, when I drum for you, you must ride the drum beat as if you were riding across the snow on a dog-sledge. Ride the drum beat far away to the heavens, ride it into the Northern Lights. Ride it among the Old Ones. Ride it down through the ice to where Nuliajuk lives with her sea creatures at the bottom of the ocean. Call out for your spirit-helpers to appear before you. Call out for your guardians and your allies. If you do this with true heart, they will come."

Sitting beside the lamp on the caribou rug, Alareak now began to sing softly to himself...a song which he

alone had the right to sing, and which he offered now
as a greeting to the spirits and the Old Ones:

> *Hunter comes forth*
> *From his sleep*
> *New day wakes*
> *With the light of dawn*
> *Hunter too will wake*
> *And journey into night…*

Rising to his feet, Alareak now held his rattle
high above his head and with bold, sweeping
gestures began to shake it to the four quarters. When
this was done he reached for his shaman-drum and
began to beat it with a small wooden drumstick.
Gradually the droning drumbeats began to gather a
momentum of their own, and increasingly Enoyuk
found himself swept along by the enchanting power
of their resonance and driving rhythm. It seemed
then that Alareak's snowhouse had itself become
like a pulsing heartbeat—a multi-layered chorus of
vibrant sounds embracing all within its confines.

Alareak and Enoyuk were now journeying together, journeying as one.

Then for a dazzling and inspiring moment, Enoyuk no longer knew where he was. Part of his being seemed now to be swept along on a tide of sound, but another part of him—his physical body, the part of him which until now he had considered his real self—seemed separate, as if it had been left behind.

Now Enoyuk felt a surge of warmth rise up within his innermost being. His soul was lifting up into the sky, flying high above Alareak's snowhouse so that he could look out far beyond Eagle's Claw, far across the shoreline to the headland in the distance. Even from this unfamiliar vantage point high up in the night sky, his spirit-eyes seemed possessed of their own inner light. This, for Enoyuk, was nothing less than a revelation: a new way of seeing which he had scarcely thought possible.

Soaring ever higher now, and rising up far beyond the imposing rocky bluff known to his people as Three Ravens, Enoyuk found himself entering a wondrous world of luminescent clouds and sprays of colored light—a world which was, perhaps, the home of helper spirits and guardians of the soul. Soon this radiance seemed to permeate every aspect of his being. He felt that he had become pure light itself, that he was radiating light, that light itself was of his very essence—the true source of his existence.

And then a spirit-creature which would become his tunraq appeared before him for the first time. He saw it faintly at first—as the glimmer of an outline, as a blur within a haze of light—but then it came closer, and soon became more tangible. Enoyuk could see then that it was a small wolf, with silvery white fur and pearly blue eyes. He had never encountered a wolf quite like this before and he had to contain his surprise at the unexpected meeting. But it was the wolf who spoke first, welcoming Enoyuk to the Land of Lights:

"I come to you as a guardian," it said, speaking with words of spirit which reached directly into Enoyuk's soul. "I offer you my intelligence, my loyalty, my skill as a hunter."

Suddenly dream-like visions appeared of the silver wolf mustering caribou into a pass where they could be ambushed by waiting hunters. Then further visions of the guardian-wolf leading other animals forth from their hiding places on the tundra. And other visions, too—of the wolf retrieving a hunter's prized harpoon lost in the snow, and seeking out seals and walruses at their breathing holes in the ice.

The wolf now told Enoyuk its true name—a name which would remain known, from this time onwards, only to its master. Finally the wolf assured Enoyuk it would always remain nearby, living at the edge of camp where it could always hear the shaman's special call, and where it would come swiftly when summoned.

Inspired by this wonderful display of allegiance, Enoyuk now gestured for the wolf to come closer and then reached forward to share breath with the spirit-animal, thanking it from his heart. "You will always be with me," said Enoyuk, "and we will share great adventures together."

Enoyuk now felt instinctively that it was time to return. He could still hear the steady beat of Alareak's drum but it seemed far away and he sought once more to immerse himself in its entrancing rhythms. But while his encounter with the silver wolf had been a wondrous one indeed, Enoyuk could hardly have anticipated the shock which would await him now.

As he drew closer to Alareak's snowhouse, retracing the path of his soul-journey with his spirit-eyes, he could see his own body slumbering peacefully on a caribou rug. At the same time, he could also see an enormous polar bear advancing aggressively toward the snow-house, brushing aside everything in its path.

The bear seemed possessed of a vast and monumental strength, moving with large, purposeful strides through the snow. When it reached Alareak's snowhouse it crushed its way with ease through the icy exterior wall, lurching inside to seize Enoyuk's sleeping body with its oustretched paws.

Even though he felt no pain—for he was far away from his body and witnessing these events only through his spirit-eyes—Enoyuk watched in horror as the bear now plunged his resting head inside its mouth, ripping away large sections of skin, hair and bone. In a savage feeding frenzy it began devouring Enoyuk's body, tearing open his fur-skin jacket as if it were of no consequence, and began to feast greedily on his flesh. Soon Enoyuk's body was a mass of blood and liquid entrails, leaching bright red stains upon the snow. Finally only Enoyuk's fractured skeleton remained.

But now an extraordinary and magical transformation took place—for just as purposefully as before, and now with a marked measure of patience and respect, the polar bear began to re-assemble Enoyuk's body…piece by piece. First it restored Enoyuk's rib-cage, skillfully aligning his bones and vertebrae in their correct positions. Then it joined Enoyuk's head, arms and legs to the torso, paying special attention to the restoration of his wounded face and skull, as well as all his shattered toes and fingers. Finally, with great care and sensitivity, it held Enoyuk's bloodied heart in its paws and breathed three long, restorative breaths over it in a way that seemed both reverent and kind—bringing new life back into the sleeping shaman's body. But even then the bear had not yet finished, for in its right paw it now produced a small piece of ivory inscribed with sacred and magical motifs—this would be the polar bear's special gift to the new shaman. Laying the sacred talisman carefully in position beside Enoyuk's heart, the bear now gently sealed the gaping, savage wound which it had earlier inflicted upon the young man's breast.

When it was all over, Enoyuk could hardly believe what he had witnessed! He had seen his own body savagely dismembered by an enormous, predatory animal but then lovingly restored, piece by piece, and returned—revitalized—to its original condition. And Enoyuk himself felt possessed of a new strength, a new energy—*a new magical potency*. He no longer feared the thought of returning from the spirit-world to his sleeping body, and there would be many wondrous things to share with his shaman-teacher when he awoke. Rising drowsily from his slumber, he now found himself once more in Alareak's presence.

Alareak had stopped drumming now, and was seated on a large caribou hide at one end of the snowhouse. It was still dim inside, as the stone lamp continued to burn with only a small flame. Alareak himself seemed very much at ease, as if nothing much of consequence had occurred. And to Enoyuk's great surprise the snowhouse itself seemed entirely intact, as if no catastrophe whatever had befallen it. There were no signs of devastation, no indications of a predatory attack, no fractures in the ice or ravaging paw marks on the walls, and no stains of blood on the snow outside. Enoyuk was deeply puzzled and alarmed. How could this be? Could he not believe the evidence of his own eyes?

Alareak watched with a wry smile upon his face as Enoyuk looked within himself for all the answers. Finally it was clear that the master shaman would have to put Enoyuk's questioning mind at ease, and explain to the young apprentice what had taken place:

"Once again, you have encountered the Great White One," he said, "and this time he has shown you his strength, his power. When he first visited you in your dream it was to tell you what was to come. Now you know he can be a feared enemy who ravages and destroys, but you have also seen that he can be a healer who rebuilds. This time he has shown you the path of healing."

"But he attacked me savagely during my soul-journey," protested Enoyuk. "He took my body apart, piece by piece."

"Yes," said Alareak. "But he also gave you your body back. And he rebuilt it, limb by limb. Soon you will feel within yourself, in the days and months ahead, that you have become a new person—a different person altogether from the one you were before. You will be a strong shaman, a brave shaman. And the Great White One has given you his gift."

Alareak now rose to his feet, draped the protective rug once again across his sacred drum, and then placed it at the back of his snowhouse for safekeeping. Turning back to Enoyuk he asked: "Tell me, what else did you experience on your journey. Did you meet your tunraq?"

"I did indeed meet my tunraq," said Enoyuk, looking reflectively toward the ceiling of the snowhouse. "And I journeyed high up in the sky to a wonderful land which glowed with the light of many lamps." Immediately Enoyuk felt the potent energy of the silver wolf rise up within his heart, and turning to face his teacher once more he began to explain the encounter in more detail. But with a sweep of his hand Alareak gestured that he should remain silent. "This is all I need to know," said Alareak. "You have journeyed far, and you have found your first tunraq. And your body, too, has been blessed and rebuilt by the Great White One. This was the purpose of your vision quest tonight."

Alareak now reached down beside his bed, producing a fine caribou belt which he offered as a gift to his young companion. "You are now a shaman in your own right," he said. "You have earned this belt, and you should wear it always as a sign of your new role in this world and the next. Remain silent when asked the name and nature of your tunraq—for in this way you guard its potency. But you should inscribe its image upon this belt and keep it with you at all times, for it is now a part of you. Every time you go upon a journey of the soul, you take its magic with you. Through your life you may gain many other tunraqs, and these too will come to you in your visions. These are the signs of a great shaman."

All of this had taken place many years ago, reflected Enoyuk, as he looked out in the dawn light from the peaceful seclusion of his snowhouse. His shaman-teacher Alareak had long since passed from this world into the land of spirits, making his way through the Northern Lights to the realm of the ancestors. Enoyuk himself was now the shaman of his community—their *angakoq*. A leader in the camp, he was greatly respected for his magical powers and for his special gift of being able to journey with the spirits to the home of the sacred ones.

Later that morning Enoyuk walked down to the center of the camp. The air was now crisp and invigorating, the snow upon the ground somewhat lighter underfoot, revealing little patches of hard grey earth. Winter, now, was surely in its last days. Soon, with the coming of spring, the ice floes would begin to melt, the sun would rise up—gathering strength as it journeyed across the sky—and a new sense of hope would come among the people.

But for now, the ravages of winter had left a lingering burden upon their hearts and minds. Many still felt anxious about the shortage of food, and the diminishing reserves of seal-fat for their lamps. Fewer seals and walruses had been taken in the hunt, and there were murmurings that Nuliajuk, Mistress of the Sea Animals, no longer sent her blessings to the hunters in the community.

Soon Enoyuk came upon his sister, Nuutlaq, who was working with a group of other women from the camp, cutting seal meat and preparing it for cooking. "This seal which Kadlajuk caught for us is much smaller than the seals which Nuliajuk used to send us in the past," she told him. Enoyuk nodded in agreement. He knew that she was a tireless worker, and that she rarely complained. Clearly she was worried that hard times still lay ahead.

For a brief moment Enoyuk stood beside her in silence, watching her admiringly as she patiently scraped the fat from the sealskin with her small round-edged knife. Then he knelt beside her, reassuring her that all would be well soon. "I will call the animals again," he said. "I know that Nuliajuk will help us."

But he also felt certain, in saying this, that various members of the camp had breached Nuliajuk's sacred laws, that their misdeeds might well be responsible for the much-diminished hunt during these long, wintery months. He had heard it whispered that on a recent hunting trip Kadlajuk had harpooned a seal without seeking permission to take its flesh for food, and that Moraq had called to the sea animals by their secret personal names—something which was sure to cause offense to the spirits. He had also heard that Tyara and Udluriak had cooked strips of dried caribou meat for their hungry children, and that they had done this on land covered with ice. Cooking the flesh of a land animal on ice was against the customs of his people. And so Enoyuk knew there would have to be a drumming—a drumming of the spirits—and that once again he would need to visit Nuliajuk.

As he walked on further through the camp, Enoyuk summoned Kadlajuk, Moraq, Tyara and Udluriak—and several others also—to come to his snowhouse that evening. There would be a calling of the spirits and Enoyuk himself would undertake a soul-journey to the stone fortress of Nuliajuk, at the bottom of the ocean. Enoyuk would ask Nuliajuk about the cause of the troubles, and urge her to release more seals and walruses into the sea for the hunters to catch. At the same time, those who had breached the sacred laws would have to confess their misdeeds. Only after they had confessed to their wrongdoings would the rift with Nuliajuk be healed. Only with her blessing would there be ample seal and walrus meat for the whole community.

Gathering the group into his snowhouse that evening, Enoyuk took off his heavy fur coat and boots. Wearing only a light undergarment, his shaman belt, and his sheathed hunting knife, he then lit his small lamp. Even with the small flickering flame it was still very dark inside. As shadows moved mysteriously across the ceiling of the snowhouse, the small gathering waited with eager anticipation.

Soon Enoyuk took out his favorite spirit-rattle and, facing in turn to each of the four directions, he now called for his tunraqs to attend.

From the north, through the shimmering darkness, came the spirit of the silver wolf—the helper-spirit which he had first encountered during his vision-quest with Alareak, and which he loved for its intelligence and its loyalty. Then, from the wintery seas to the east, Enoyuk summoned his walrus-spirit—a tunraq prized for its strength and courage beneath the crashing ice-floes. From the tundra in the south came the spirit of a polar bear—not the Great White One which had destroyed and rebuilt his body during his vision-quest but another spirit known only by its secret name: "The One without a Shadow." This bear-spirit he had taken as his ally for its persistence and agility both on land and in the water—for polar bears are not only great hunters and stalkers, but can also swim strongly in icy waters. And finally, from the snow-capped rocky crags in the west Enoyuk called his white winter-owl, a helper-spirit with a haunting night-time call. This spirit had mastery over death and would help in those unforeseen times when life itself was threatened.

Enoyuk now began to beat steadily on his drum, singing his most potent shaman-songs and building a vibrant tunnel of sound through which he could journey in his spirit-vision. At first his songs and invocations seemed to find their focus within the very center of the gathering, and the snowhouse filled with an eerie silver-blue light. Then, before the watchful gaze of everyone assembled, the column of sound began to gather a dramatic momentum of its own, transforming from a thundering rhythm into a great vortex of water—a swirling tunnel through which Enoyuk could travel to the very depths of the ocean.

And now, protected from all four directions by his helper-spirits, Enoyuk disappeared suddenly from view. A splashing, gurgling sound was all that lingered in his absence, and everyone knew that Enoyuk had departed on his spirit-journey to the home of Nuliajuk, Goddess of the Sea.

Enoyuk had visited Nuliajuk before. On several occasions in times past, Alareak had led him on this spirit-journey down through the swirling depths of the ocean—bringing him finally to the portal of Nuliajuk's stone fortress. Alareak had shown him the secret path which led past the three large boulders which marked the entrance to her spirit-home. He had learned not to fear the giant guard-dog which lay waiting at the door for unwanted intruders. Afterward, having entered Nuliajuk's secret abode, he had watched in awe as Alareak enchanted the sea-goddess with his sacred songs.

This time Enoyuk hoped that the spirit of Alareak would once again guide him on his quest, for it was always wonderful to feel the presence of departed friends and teachers. He felt sure that he possessed the magical strength and knowledge to persuade Nuliajuk to help his people. And much depended on her support, for without the blessing of Nuliajuk, the sea creatures would hide within the depths of the ocean and the people would go hungry.

In the very deepest part of the ocean, Enoyuk came finally to the island where Nuliajuk and the sea animals had built her stone fortress. This was a secret place, for only the shamans with their spirit-vision knew that at the very bottom of the ocean there was yet another land—a land of sea, earth and sky—and that it was here, from her stone fortress, that Nuliajuk could look out and witness the ways of the world above.

Striding boldly up to the gate of the fortress, Enoyuk brushed aside the snarling dog which guarded the entrance. Once inside, he found Nuliajuk seated in the middle of a large room, accompanied by several of her sea creatures. Her face was turned away, for she sat with her back toward the door. Enoyuk did not wait for her to acknowledge him, and announced his presence immediately:

"I am Enoyuk, and I am flesh and blood," he said

boldly. "And I have come to your spirit-home to urge you to help my people."

Nuliajuk now turned to face him. She knew in her heart what had brought this shaman to her home. She knew that on their journeys of the soul, shamans only ever came to visit her when their world was deeply troubled—when spirits of hunger and sickness roamed across the land.

Nuliajuk knew also that her mastery of the sea bestowed vast power over the hunters and their prey. But she nevertheless feared the shaman's knife—for she too had once dwelt among the living, and she too had once been brutalized. Memories flooded back of her cruel father severing her fingers as she clung desperately to the side of their small boat.

Containing the fears which still lingered in her heart, Nuliajuk now spoke to Enoyuk about the nature of his quest: "I know you are of the people," she said. "I know you are a being of flesh and blood—for I saw you approach from the land of the living. And I know full well that your people are hungry, that there are fewer seals and walruses in the sea for your hunters to catch. I have kept many of these creatures here with me, for I am angered by the actions of certain people in your camp."

Nuliajuk continued, before Enoyuk could respond to her:

"Look at the grime which has washed down from your people, and which has left its dark stains upon my body. These particles of silt are the misdeeds—the breaches of sacred law—which have defiled the ways of being that were taught to us by the Ancient Ones. As a respected *angakoq* and leader you must surely know that different members of your camp have gone against the sacred teachings, that they have done things they should not have done."

Enoyuk learned then that Kadlajuk, Moraq, Tyara and Udluriak had caused deep offense to the Mistress of the Sea Animals and he felt a deep sadness within himself. He felt the hurt and violation which his people had inflicted upon this Goddess of the Sea, this sacred protector who had sustained them all through the seasons of their lives. No longer could he press his demands upon Nuliajuk through strength or aggression, or through the threatening presence of his hunting knife. Instead, a new compassion seized his heart as he sought to appease and enchant her, rather than conquer her with forceful persuasion.

There was beauty still within Nuliajuk, but the misdeeds of the people had ravaged her skin and brought a weariness to her body with the passing of the years. Her eyes were now full of sadness, for her soul bore the full burden of a world long torn by the ways of human deception. As fate had decreed, Nuliajuk now had no fingers to wipe away her tears— for her severed fingers had become the seals and whales and walruses which found protection in her secret domain. But she too was in need of human care.

Taking her comb in his hand, Enoyuk now began to draw it gently through her matted hair, untangling the knots and allowing long strands to flow carefree across her back. Then, with tender, loving movements he began to wash the grime of human wrongdoings from her stained and ravaged body.

And now from within his soul there arose won-drous, magical songs—songs which had been given to him by his teacher and which he now sang to enchant Nuliajuk, reassuring her that he had come to visit her with peaceful intent. His songs were songs of the birth of the land from the waters...songs of the healing of the world and its peoples...songs of sea creatures sacrificing themselves within the everlasting cycle of life and death so that human beings could be nourished and live in harmony with the world. Finally, when it was all over, Nuliajuk assured Enoyuk that she would bless his camp, and that large numbers of seals and walruses would once again be released into the ocean.

Enoyuk thanked Nuliajuk for her kindness and now took his leave of the Sea Goddess and her creatures. Returning to the pebbly foreshore, he plunged into the lapping waves to make his way home.

Soon he found the spirit-pathway which joined Nuliajuk's world with his—the swirling watery tunnel which would bring him back from the depths of the ocean, past menacing boulders of floating ice, to the familiar presence of his snowhouse.

Rising swiftly toward the surface, Enoyuk could

now hear in the distance the expectant voices of his comrades. And he could see his loyal tunraqs guarding the entrance of his spirit-tunnel from each of the four directions. Finally he passed through the thick layers of earth and ice beneath his snowhouse, and with a call of joyous exultation once again took his place in the very center of the shaman-gathering.

Warmly greeted on his safe return, Enoyuk now rested on a caribou blanket as his friends sat around him in hushed silence. "The Great Goddess Nuliajuk has heard our call," he told them. "I have journeyed to visit her in the very depths of the ocean. I have ventured to the stone fortress where only an *angakoq* may visit, and I have entered the innermost room of her secret dwelling. I have braided her hair and cleansed her body, and I have sung to her the sacred songs our people. And I say to you now that Nuliajuk has heard our call and will send more seals and walruses into the ocean so we may, once again, have sufficient food for the coming season."

Enoyuk now paused for a moment, in order to deliver the full impact of his message.

"But she has also decreed," he continued, "that all of those who have gone against the sacred laws must confess their wrongdoings. Each of you here who have broken the teachings of the ancient ones must make amends now. Each of you, in turn, must confess to your misdeeds."

Shadows flickered across the ceiling of the snow-house as Kadlajuk now came forward from the group to confess that he had indeed harpooned a seal without first seeking permission to take it in the hunt. Then Moraq confessed that he too had gone against the ancient teaching of the animal spirits and had called the sea creatures by their secret personal names. Finally Tyara and Udluriak confessed that they had cooked strips of dried caribou meat for their hungry children, and that they had done this on land covered with ice—which was against the customs of the people. And each in turn begged for forgiveness, beseeching the spirits to accept their deeply felt regret, so that Nuliajuk would continue in the coming seasons to send her blessings to the camp.

With the passing of winter into spring, a more peaceful and joyous feeling came upon the people. The ice floes began to melt around their edges, and in the places where the ice was thin, the hunters were now able to spear char through the ice as well as catching seals and walruses from their kayaks. The people were pleased and grateful that Nuliajuk once again favored them with her blessings.

Then, early one morning, there came a sacred sign—a portent from the distant world beyond the Land of Lights. Enoyuk was walking alone on the foreshore, toward the headland known as Three Ravens. Absorbed in thought, he reflected on a good time to call his people together, a good time to move the winter camp inland to firmer ground. But now his attention was seized by something altogether different.

At first he heard only a wonderful song, a lilting spirit-song unlike anything he had heard before. The song was one of great beauty, a beauty far beyond the songs of humankind. It seemed to rise up from the snow-capped rocky outcrops which lined the foreshore, but in truth it belonged to no place on this earth. Enoyuk felt its harmonies resonate within him, comforting him with a great sense of belonging and renewal. And then, as he felt increasingly enraptured by the beauty of this song, he saw that the song itself had called forth a circle of silver-white light—and that his four tunraqs were also part of this sacred circle.

Hovering in the sky, just above the circle of light, he could see the glistening outline of his white winter-owl. On the left of the circle was his loyal walrus-spirit, and on the right the bear-guardian he knew only as "The One without a Shadow." And on a snow-capped rock just beneath the light, guarding the glowing circle as if it were a sacred doorway, Enoyuk saw his silver wolf—the spirit-ally which had first come to him from the Land of Lights, and which now held a special place within his heart. And the wolf was calling him, calling him to come closer— calling him to enter the circle of light and undertake a sacred journey. They would travel together to the home of the Ancient Ones.

As Enoyuk approached the sacred circle he knew within his heart that this journey would be like no other he had ever undertaken. And still the silver wolf was calling him, calling him upon this sacred quest. As the *angakoq* of his people Enoyuk could not deny this call. Trusting that his spirit-ally had indeed come as a messenger from the Ancient Ones, Enoyuk passed through the radiant hoop of light, following his silver wolf while his other tunraqs stayed behind to guard the entrance. And still the sacred song was resonating within him, enchanting him with its beauty, and revitalizing him with its power.

Immediately he knew that he was entering another time and place. For now he was moving swiftly through a transparent tunnel of glistening light, a tunnel somehow distinct from the waking world beyond. He was sure now that he was seeing with his spirit-eyes for he could not feel the weight of his body, nor glimpse the shape of his physical form—and yet everything around him he could see quite clearly, even to the furthest horizon. And still the silver wolf moved ahead in the distance, turning every now and then to see that he was following.

Although he felt no wind upon his face, Enoyuk sensed now that he was moving rapidly—flying over vast tracts of partly melted snow, over large stretches of barren tundra, and over lakes and mountains which he had never seen before. And now he seemed to be rising high into the sky, toward the Land of Lights itself, flying to a world whose pathways were illumined by the glowing lamps and torches of the departed ones.

He seemed now to be approaching a campsite—for away in the distance he could glimpse a cluster of snowhouses and snow-tents similar to those he had recently left behind. This camp seemed somehow familiar, and as he drew closer he could see that a small group of people was gathering to welcome him. They were sheathed in the radiance of a hundred silver moons.

Then, to his great surprise, he saw that his beloved mother, Seelaki, was here and so too his father, Kaormik—both of whom had passed across into the spirit-world some years before. And his shaman-teacher Alareak was here as well. He looked unchanged, with his strong, aloof presence, and a face which spoke of wisdom earned through many trials and seasons.

All three greeted him with great joy, and it was wonderful to see them all again. But just as Enoyuk paused to embrace them each in turn, he was summoned yet again. For the sacred song was calling him once more, propelling him on wings of spirit to a world far beyond the land of human souls. Soon their faces disappeared from view, melting in a haze of light. And still the silver wolf moved on ahead, urging Enoyuk at every turn to make haste and follow in its tracks.

Now he could see rising up before him a vast luminescent cloud, which stretched for the full width of the horizon. Rising up within this cloud were three snow-capped mountain peaks, one higher than the others. And on the tallest of these three peaks there stood a sacred being, and this was Sila, Lord of the Air. Enoyuk knew then that he had indeed been summoned to the land of the Ancient Ones, a land which had always existed, even before the coming of the seasons—before the waters and the sky and the people in this world had come into being. For it was Sila himself who breathed the life-force into each new creature born upon this earth. It was Sila who controlled the great forces of the sky, summoning fierce snowstorms and hostile weather when he was angered by the people. And it was Sila too who sent the spirit of his whole being to enter the earth when he felt happy. At those times the weather would be calm, and the strong winds would abate.

And as Enoyuk looked upon Sila he was awesome to behold, for he was sheathed in a cloak of rustling wind and his ancient craggy face was like a pummelled rock, long weathered by the storms. His eyes were like bolts of silver lightning, and his deep voice spoke of untamed winds and tempests, as well as of new life filled with hope and possibility. And it was he who had summoned Enoyuk to come before him, as the *angakoq* of his people.

Now Sila addressed him in words of spirit which flowed like a stream of breath into every pore of his being. Sila told him then that the world was yet again heading for a time of fierce storms and turbulence, and that the Ancient Ones were greatly angered by the ways of the people. That hunters no longer obeyed the sacred teachings, and that mothers and young ones too had overlooked the customs they had learned. That men now went abroad only with wickedness and cunning in their hearts, and that in all lands upon the earth the people had turned their faces far away from the Ancient Ones whose gift of life had been bestowed with a good spirit and a loving intent. And now that the people could no longer place their bond of trust with one another, the very song of life had vanished from their hearts.

But there would be a cleansing, a renewal, a coming forth of a new world from the old. Trusted *angakoqs* from each of the four directions would be summoned by the Ancient Ones to the very center of the world. And here the Great Song of Life would rise up once again, and the great Gods and Goddesses from all regions of the heavens, sea and earth would unite and bestow their blessings one last time upon the people of all lands—for this was the only way forward. And he, Enoyuk, had been chosen to be present at the rebirth of the world.

Sila now indicated that Enoyuk should accompany him alone, and the loyal silver wolf who had brought him to this sacred place should make the journey home.

Lifted by a swift stream of air, Sila and Enoyuk now journeyed together through the sky. And soon they had ventured far beyond the snow-capped mountain peaks of Sila's realm, far beyond the Land of Lights and far beyond the land of human souls—to a world unknown by humankind.

This was the land of the Beginning, the land of the first times—a place which had always been, even before the first oceans, rocks and mountains had come to be. For in this place, in timeless seasons long past, the great Gods and Goddesses from all regions of the heavens had come together to build a world of earth and sky and sea. And this world then was filled with all manner of plants and living creatures, so that— from this time onward—it would become the home for all of humankind. The great Gods and Goddesses had given their blessing for this to be so, and this is how the world had come to be.

But now, as Sila had said, the world was entering dark and turbulent times and the great Gods and Goddesses had seen that this was coming. And they had decreed that the Great Song of Life should rise up yet again, so that once more—and without delay—the world could be renewed. The world would once again receive the blessing of the Ancient Ones.

And so it was that Sila brought his trusted shaman—his *angokoq*, Enoyuk—down from the sky to a place known as the Great Lake of Spirit, that vast inland sea which lies at the very center of the world—the eternal lake from which All Things Come Forth. Beside this lake Sila and Enoyuk would wait until the appointed time, knowing that in other lands, too, the Ancient Ones had also gone in search of loyal and worthy messengers. And in all quarters their purpose would be the same—to send forth a sacred song which would be heard by one entrusted to hear its call.

For this was the nature of the quest: that from each of the four directions—from North, South, East and West—these shamans of the sacred song would come forth as custodians of the Great Spirit and journey to this sacred place. And they too would serve as witnesses to the rebirth of the world.

SOUTH

Toward nightfall Kalu went back to the cave where he had hidden his churinga and his other secret possessions. Inside, the cave felt safe and welcoming. Here Kalu felt as if he had burrowed within the earth itself, close to the spirits and close to the Earth Mother. He had chosen this cave because its entrance was only visible high up on the rocky bluff, its opening accessible only from the top of a large sentinel rock which jutted out above the red-earth desert below. It was a secret place, and Kalu knew his precious churinga could be safely hidden here.

From this position Kalu could see way off into the distance, beyond the white-bark river gums which lined the freshwater stream below, beyond the patches of spinifex and tussock grass, to the purple-tinged mountains which marked the horizon. This was the land of the Lizard Dreaming—his own Dreaming. He was the safekeeper of this land. This was his country— and his father's country before him—and he was its custodian. He had looked after this land since his father, Talpu, had made him into a man at the time of his initiation.

Kalu remembered how, at that time, red-hot coals had been pressed hard against his skin leaving searing marks across his body. He remembered the agonizing pain—and also the need for silence—as his foreskin was cut back tightly by a sharp blade. But then, when that was over, Talpu had taken him along sacred paths marked upon the earth. These were the tracks where their Spirit Ancestor had walked in the dawn of the first time, that sacred time when the spirit-powers of Creation had shaped this land and when the Law had first come into being. Talpu had shown him where the Lizard Ancestor had found food on its journey, where it had created rock ridges and burrowing holes, and where it had paused to rest. He had shown him where it performed the special dance of the lizard spirits and where a song had come forth from the spinifex, which all lizards knew as their own song. And they had come to the place where the Lizard Ancestor had then burrowed deep within the earth, like all small burrowing lizards do today. This was where the Ancestor had its sacred home, even now.

For Kalu knew that even though the first dawn of Creation took place in timeless seasons past, the Tjukurrpa was with his people still—for the Dreaming was everywhere. It was in the rocks and in the earth, and in the waterholes and creeks. It was in the plants and in the birds and in all the animals of the hunt. It was in the sky and in the clouds, and in the seasons which brought rain and new growth. And it was in all of his people too, for they were custodians of Dreamings all across the land—from the furthest wind-swept coastal shores, to the fertile valleys and arid inland deserts. Kalu knew that the Dreaming spoke the Law within every human soul and he knew too, as all his people had known before him, that it was his responsibility to care for this land, for he himself had come forth from the land and belonged to it—its flesh was his flesh. He knew that through his custodianship of the sacred ways the seasons of the future would flow forth with abundance. And this would come about with the blessing of the Spirit Ancestors.

As the dark shadows of night came down upon the rock cave, Kalu made a small campfire near the entrance—both for light and for warmth—and then went inside, where he had previously lain some old blankets for his bedding. At the back of the cave, Kalu had hidden his flat-faced stone churinga— the sacred talisman which had been given to him when he first became a man. Holding it reverently in his hands, Kalu once again explored every small detail of its secret markings, every small symbol which told the tale of his Spirit Ancestor and the journey undertaken during the Creation of the World.

And now Kalu felt the sacred lizard-song rise up within him, nourishing him with its stories of the earth and the different paths of power across the land.

For Kalu knew those secret places—places where the power of the spirit would burst forth from the red earth with a rumbling of thunder that he knew was the voice of the Spirit Ancestor. And he knew too where one country ended and another began, where the life-sustaining songs of different spirit-countries had their boundaries, and where the songs of one people would join with those of another.

Kalu knew that all of the land was like a mesh of songs, woven into the very fabric of the earth, and that each custodian had just a small and special part to watch over. But his country—the land of the Lizard Dreaming—was the country where the Ancestors had decreed that his hunting would be done, where large animals could be speared for food and taken back to camp. Kalu knew that as long as he carried the song of his churinga within his heart, the hunting would be good. Sooner or later, if he was patient, the larger animals would come—maybe an emu, or a grey kangaroo, or a rock wallaby— and there would be good food for his family back at the camp.

At daybreak Kalu came down from the rock ledge
with his spears and wooden club, wearing only his
purdurru hair-string belt and a length of cloth around
his forehead to protect his eyes from the blistering
sun. Crossing the creek like a silent warrior, he made
his way past the white-bark river gums, striding bare-
foot across the sandy foothills to the men's camp. He
was meeting his skin-brother Winjin, and they would
go off to hunt together.

When Kalu arrived at the camp, Winjin was
already preparing to depart, and soon the two men
were heading off through the mulga country in the
direction of the Wirringi soak—a rock pool where
many animals would come to drink, and where the
hunting would be good. Like Kalu, Winjin was a
lizard man, and as brothers of the same skin they
could hunt together on the same land. Winjin was
also the custodian of country which had come to him
from his mother's people—but that was far away, past
Arimala to the west. Here in the lizard-country both
men knew the same Dreaming tracks, the same secret
stories of the Spirit Ancestor, and the same lizard-

songs and dances which had been given to them long ago—when they had been made into men by the elders of the camp.

As they came through the sandhill country, Kalu watched closely for markings on the red earth— broken strands of grass, clusterings of footprints, scattered leaves and seed-pods. He had worked for a time as a tracker in these bushlands and he knew the country well. And he knew too the fruits, roots and seeds which could be taken as food to sustain them on the hunt.

But it was Winjin who first saw the grey kangaroo—far away in the distance, in the direction of the soak. A large and handsome creature, it had frozen in its tracks as it sensed their approach and was anxiously surveying the bushlands for signs of an attack. Winjin knew how to "sing" the animal into submission and as he sent forth the song of the hunt he knew too that the grey kangaroo had heard this song as well, and had become transfixed by its power. Soon Winjin was close enough to see the animal clearly and, moving still closer, he engaged it eye to eye and held its threatened gaze with all the spirit-strength he could muster. Then, with a mighty and all-conquering thrust, Winjin let fly with his spear, striking the kangaroo through its chest and felling it immediately to the ground.

As they stood beside the fallen animal, Winjin and Kalu gave thanks for the gift which had been given to them by the Spirit Ancestors. This was a large creature, a finely built adult male with a full body and a heavy tail, and its meat would provide sustenance for many nights to come. Draping the carcass across two gumtree poles, and heaving its weight across their shoulders, the two men prepared to carry the grey kangaroo back to the camp.

There were two groupings of bark-shelters at the campsite—one for the men, and the other for the women and young children—and they lived apart around the campfire. Like all the men, Winjin and Kalu knew that women's business was not their affair, that the women had their sacred ways which belonged to them alone, just as there were men's ways that were for men only—as the Law had decreed. But gathering food was a task in which they all shared, and while Winjin and Kalu had been away hunting for larger prey, some of the women had also been foraging for bush-tucker—digging for wild potato with their coolamons and mulga sticks. By nightfall Winjin's wife Jorna had brought in a good pile of yams which could be roasted on the coals of the campfire, while her sister Biddy and the children had gathered an assortment of juicy witchetty grubs and a cluster of small bush tomatoes. Kalu's young wife Tilo had been away gathering seeds and wild plums.

As the campfire blazed high into the night sky that evening, the food was good and there was enough for all, and they gave thanks that the Spirit Ancestors had blessed them yet again. For a time Kalu played games in the red dirt with his eldest boy Jiri, who would soon be of an age for the first rites of passage—rites that would take him toward being made into a man. And Kalu also spent precious time with Tilo, reassuring her that although it was not the men's way to make public shows of affection at the campsite, he cared for her greatly. For it was true that Kalu held a special place for her in his heart, even though his hunting journeys sometimes kept them apart for many days and nights at a time.

Then Kalu hummed a song which Tilo remembered from the time, several seasons past, when they had first made love together—close by the waterhole at the edge of camp. And the spirit-children who had been placed in the waterhole by the Spirit Ancestors had come up inside her, and had brought new life within her, and soon she had discovered that she was with child. And this she knew—that the Spirit Ancestors had decreed that she and Kalu should be man and woman together, and the group at the camp had also seen that this should be.

But soon Kalu would be leaving again. The day after the hunt brought an unexpected shower of rain, and on the following day three yellow flowers sprang forth in a line from the red earth—pointing in the direction of Kalu's spirit-country. Kalu knew this was a sign, a sign that he had been called by the Spirit Ancestor and would have to make a journey, alone, to the land of his birth.

Bidding farewell to Tilo and Jiri and his other friends in the camp, Kalu now set off for his spirit-country with his hunting weapons—on a journey which would take him away from his family for several days and nights. First he would return to his secret cave to retrieve his churinga, and then he would journey further north, following the sacred markings upon the rocks and earth, and protected after sunset by the great sky-spirits whose home was in the depths of night. Kalu knew there were hostile spirits in the bushland, especially in the creeks and waterholes of the neighbouring custodial lands through which he would have to pass—and vengeful spirits might seek to surprise or attack him. But the power of the lizard-song was deep within his heart, and was always there to guide him. Kalu felt sure that the spirits would help him on the journey, and he knew he would feel even stronger with his churinga at his side.

Striding briskly from the camp, Kalu soon crossed the creek and passed by the white-bark river gums. Tracking through the spinifex country and making his way past patches of tussock grass and mulga, he could soon pick out the distinctive shape of the sentinel rock, outlined against the sky. A band of red and green lorikeets flew past to greet him with their raucous call, and soon he was climbing over large boulders to scale the rock-face leading to his cave.

Everything was as he had left it—except for one thing. Near the entrance to his cave, marked out carefully in white feathers upon the dark red earth, was the most sacred sign from his churinga—a symbol which the Spirit Ancestors themselves had given him, many seasons past. And yet Kalu did not feel the presence of human intruders, for nothing else had been touched. His churinga was still safely hidden at the back of the cave, and had not been disturbed. And in every other way Kalu felt assured that only good spirits—helper spirits—had been here. So he took it to be a special calling, a sign that the Ancestors had marked this out as a special journey to his spirit-country.

Armed with his churinga and his hunting weapons Kalu now came down from the rock ledge and headed in a direction which would take him some distance from the camp—toward the purple-tinged mountains which marked the southern song-track of his sacred Lizard Dreaming.

Keen to reach his spirit-land before the onset of darkness, Kalu made his way across the stony outcrop known as Nallelunga and then passed along a dry creek bed between tall cliffs which for a time shielded him from the fierce heat of the sun. Then he came upon a swampy rock-pool with black herons, but was keen to pass by quickly, for he knew that hostile spirits might dwell in a place like this.

Beyond the rock-pool were groups of large red-bark gums and acacias, and clusters of small white and purple flowers scattered through long, feathery grasses. Soon Kalu was climbing higher, scaling large, weathered boulders which had marked this rock-ridge pathway from the time when the Spirit Ancestors had first journeyed through this land. Passing across the top of the ridge and tracking toward the foothills in the distance, Kalu could see now that his spirit-land was not far off. And with every bold stride, he could feel the song of the lizard-spirits becoming ever stronger, rising from the earth to greet him.

The sun shone low in the sky as Kalu arrived at the edge of his spirit country. Red-tinged golden light fell in hallowed swathes across the weathered rocks and Kalu knew that the Ancient Ones were here. This was a land of spirits and Ancestors and departed ones, a land blessed by the Tjukurrpa and honored by his people ever since. It was a place where the Dreaming was strong, and where magical life-force—kurunpa— seemed to pour from the earth like a healing balm. It was a place where the trees and birds and rock ledges called forth their song, a place where one's soul was bonded to the very earth itself. Above all, it was a place for listening, a place where the stories of the earth were shared once again—spoken by the spirits and the Ancient Ones who had known the meanings of these stories since earliest times.

Then, in the fading light of dusk, Kalu came face to face with the Lizard Man himself. Shiny scales adorned his silver body, his fingers were tipped with sharped, pointed claws, and a long tail draped itself across nearby rocks like a liquid cloak. The Lizard Man stood proud and erect, his light-filled eyes alive with the songs of the Dreaming. And he was "singing" Kalu now, pouring into him the healing power of the Lizard Ancestor, an ancient song of magical power—a song which had once been sung to shape the very land itself, filling it with sacred meaning.

Looking down, Kalu could see now that in every way he had become a lizard man himself—a true custodian of the Dreaming. For he no longer wore the dusty, sun-parched skin of a simple hunter but was clothed instead in the glistening, silken skin of a reptilean god. He felt his face stretch and grow, and it was becoming more elongated, more pointed. He reached to touch his dry mouth and suddenly felt a darting lizard's tongue. He saw now with lizard's eyes, and heard with lizard's ears. And still the stories of the Lizard Dreaming were unfolding deep within his soul, with all the twists and undulations of a lizard burrowing deep within the earth. The Dreaming was telling him that still greater lessons lay ahead, that he would venture into new worlds and meet spirit-helpers and allies as yet unknown to him. And also that he would meet again with the Crystal Father, the revered Spirit of the Sky who ruled the earth from his home beyond the clouds.

Now Kalu brought forth his sacred churinga, to show it to the Lizard Man. And the Lizard Man was pleased that he had been shown this secret sign of custodianship, for he and Kalu were born of the same Ancestor. Soon the secret markings upon the stone talisman began to glisten and overflow with light—even as Kalu held it in his hand—and he knew he was protected in this ancient land, watched over by guardian spirits who would help him on his quest.

Watching him keenly with his alert, light-filled eyes, the Lizard Man now reminded Kalu of his obligations—that early the following day he should make his way to the sacred rock of the lizard spirits, where lizards were waiting to be born. Kalu should cut his arm, letting his blood flow down upon this rock, to bring life to the lizard spirits and allow them to come forth into this world. And then he would sing the ancient lizard-song and dance the lizard-dance, as had always been done since earliest times.

At daybreak, with pale golden light filtering across the sacred ceremonial ground and illuminating the tip of lizard-rock, Kalu performed the things expected of him as a custodian of the land. Sounding his clapper sticks and dancing hard upon the ground as he made his calls, he knew that once again—through the power of his songs and his sacred dance—the lizard country would be renewed and made fertile and abundant with the blessing of the sacred ones. Meanwhile the Lizard Man watched on, and was greatly pleased by Kalu's sacred bond of trust. For Kalu had been tutored in these ways by his father Talpu, and Talpu by his father before him, and these teachings of the Law would continue as the Spirit Ancestors had decreed.

The Lizard Man now told Kalu that he had a message for him from the Ancient Ones: that he had been chosen from all the elders in his camp to become a "clever man"—a shaman and a healer for his people—and this was a reward for his honor and his trust. And he would know when this was about to take place because the Crystal Father himself would visit Kalu unannounced, from a place beyond the clouds. There would be ordeals to go through, and lessons to be learned, but as a shaman he would journey still further in the world of gods and spirits.

Then, before Kalu could express his surprise or seek answers to his questions, the Lizard Man was gone. And Kalu was left to ponder on the wondrous nature of his spirit-country, and the strange and mysterious beings who dwelt here.

There were other Dreamings in this land as well, for secret song-tracks meshed across the earth in all directions and different creatures had their tales and ancient songs to sing, songs which had flowed into the red earth when it still was young. So Kalu surveyed his spirit-country well, paying homage to the golden bandicoots in the north, dancing the writhing dance of the carpet snake in the west, and performing sacred arm-blood rituals for the spirits of the wombats in the east. In the southern bushlands he sang once again the secret songs of the desert oak, and honored the three yellow flowers which had sprouted from the red earth. And then, on the second day, as he prepared to leave his spirit country, Kalu returned to the very center of his custodial land—to the spirit rock of the Lizard Dreaming—and here once again he danced the dances and sang the songs which would allow the lizard-spirits to come forth and make their homes within the living earth.

Toward the end of the second day, and allowing time for the journey home, Kalu turned once again toward the purple mountains which marked the southern boundary of his spirit-country. Moving through the bushland and greeted at every turn by small animals which scurried around his feet, Kalu came finally to the rock-ridge pathway which had been made by the Spirit Ancestors in the Dreaming time. He then descended across the large, weathered boulders which he had scaled just a few days earlier, and continued on his way. Soon he found himself among a familiar group of red-bark gums and acacias, and then he came upon clusters of small white and purple flowers scattered through long, feathery grasses. And he knew then that he was close to home.

The sun was now low in the sky, casting long blue-grey shadows across the land, as Kalu came once again to the swampy rock-pool where he had seen the black herons on his journey north. Once again he was keen to pass by quickly, for he knew that hostile spirits might dwell here in a place like this.

In the distance he could see the tall cliffs rising on either side of the dry creek bed and he remembered how, just a few days before, those towering rocks had shielded him from the fierce heat of the sun. But now the shadows were lengthening still further across the gumtrees and the red earth. And the track between the towering cliffs would be hard to find as darkness threatened to come down rapidly upon the land.

Soon a thought came to Kalu that he had not allowed sufficient time for the journey home, and an uneasy fear began to gnaw at him inside. But still he felt the power of his churinga and the reassuring presence of his hunting weapons, and he remembered that the Lizard Man had promised to protect him as he ventured into unknown lands beyond the domain of his spirit-ancestors.

But now darkness shrouded the tall cliffs with the threat of unseen things, as Kalu sought to make his way carefully along the sharp, uneven rocks of the dry creek bed. Strange and eerie whisperings sounded deep within the rock-face, and echoed through the pass as he moved uneasily ahead. A solitary black crow darted from one high rock to another while looking down upon him, and Kalu wondered whether he had come unawares to the homeland of the dead.

Still the darkness confronted him, and still he felt the fear rise up inside. As the clammy night air brushed menacingly across his face, Kalu clutched his churinga still closer to his chest and grasped his hunting weapons ever more tightly—so tightly that his clenched fist soon felt frozen to his spears. And a stream of salty sweat began to flow into his eyes.

Then, in a soft whisper—a whisper which made the hairs rise up upon his neck—a voice spoke to him.

"It is good that you have come," the voice told him, "for there is much that we must do."

Shrouded by the darkness, Kalu had no sense of whether this was an enemy or a friend. But then the voice spoke once more, and again its whispered tones reached deep into his heart: "Do not fear," the voice was telling him, "for certain things will happen now, but they will open your soul to the ways of the spirit. You will pass through Earth and Water, Fire and Air— and this will make you then into a new man, a 'clever man.' But you must face the fears which are gathering in your heart and pass them by, like a true warrior of the Dreaming."

Kalu felt sure that this must be the Crystal Father speaking with him now. Surely this was the great Sky Spirit who would come unannounced from a place beyond the stars? Surely this was the meeting which the Dreaming had foretold? But then a sense of deep unease came over him, for in the eerie darkness of the night nothing could be seen and nothing could be certain. Perhaps these whisperings were the taunts of an evil spirit who had come instead to deceive him?

But then, before he could respond to what he had been told, Kalu was seized by unseen forces, and his arms and shoulders were thrust roughly behind his back. Drawn forcibly along the narrow uneven track, Kalu stumbled as his feet slipped on the sharp rocks and his spears and churinga fell to the ground, rolling away in the darkness. And now, before he could pause to retrieve them, he was swept along ever more swiftly, his body reeling from the pain and terror inflicted by invisible assailants.

With a sense of impending dread, Kalu felt sure he was being taken back to the swampy rock hole where he had first seen the black herons—a place, no doubt, where evil ghosts and spirits lurked beneath the reeds. And now he was being beaten and pummeled, and long spears were being thrust into his body, slicing painfully into his flesh. He was falling into pieces, falling into small fragments, and these pieces of his body were being thrown—one by one—into the swampy pool where they could be taken as food by the black herons.

But still he seemed to have a spirit-body that remained unharmed—even if his other body had now been torn and sliced to pieces. And as he looked down upon the fragments of his shattered body, he was amazed to find that in his spirit-vision he could rise above this wounded shell, gliding swiftly like a leaf in the stream, darting between small stones at the bottom of the pool, swimming between the stems of tall reeds which reached up into the sky.

But if his spirit-vision was like a fleeting gift of freedom, he now felt a sudden surge of searing pain as burning coals were thrust against him—a deeply wounding pain that ravaged every part of his being, scalding his heart and torching the furthest corners of his soul. For this was no ordinary attack, no ordinary magic. Soon flames were leaping high into the night and even ravaging the rock-pool itself, consuming its waters with a savage thirst so fierce that now even the pool ran dry, and only molten, steaming rocks remained behind. And all this time Kalu had wanted to scream in agony, but he knew he must remain silent, as a mark of bravery and strength.

Soon a cool and healing breeze came down upon him, and a stream of soft air swept across his spirit-body like a healing balm. And it was soothing him, placating him—reassuring him that his body had been made whole again, and that he had indeed been born anew from earth and fire and water.

Now he was rising up, a formless spirit in the air, floating high above the rock-pool of the black herons which somehow had magically reappeared. And now he saw that different creatures had come to watch over him, to strengthen his resolve and guard his passage through the spirit-world. And these were the creatures of his spirit-country. To the north he saw his golden bandicoot, a sign of good luck, and to the west, outlined against the night sky, a writhing carpet snake, which shared with him the sacred colors of its Dreaming. And from the east had come his brown wombat—a friend with sacred knowledge of the seeds and fruits and grasses of the earth.

Then, in the south, Kalu saw a creature that at first he did not recognize for it was sheathed in the velvet mist of dusk. But then he could see that this was the sacred dingo of the purple mountains, a guardian of the Dreaming track which marked the southern entrance to his spirit-country. And it too had come here as a spirit-ally for his journeys of the soul.

Rising still higher in his spirit-vision, rising like a wisp of spiraling smoke, Kalu began to feel the soothing caress of silver light flowing down from the sky, filling his soul as if it were a hollow vessel. He could see that the light was like a fine sheen of liquid quartz, and that it flowed from a mantle high up in the heavens, a place where the Sky God had made his home amidst the stars.

Now a wondrous song was sounding through the heavens, and it was nurturing his soul and telling him that his trial of fear was ended. And a haze of mellow dew-filled light fell down around him as Kalu came now before the Crystal Father, guardian of the sacred Law. The Crystal Father was awesome to behold, for his body shone with silver light. Quartz crystals flowed in a stream from his long beard, filling the heavens with glistening stars.

Now the Crystal Father reached down to Kalu, holding forth his right hand in a gesture of peace. Within his hand he held a piece of shining quartz, and once again Kalu heard the gentle whispering tones that he had heard earlier, in the valley of the night. "This is your new heart," said the Crystal Father. "This is the heart of a true healer."

With these words the Crystal Father placed the shining quartz deep within Kalu's chest. And soon he could feel its pulse and sense that new life had been given to him, for silver light coursed through his body where once red blood had flowed. Now the Crystal Father was telling him that a new spirit dwelt within him, that he would be known as a healer and a shaman from this time forth. And once he returned to camp, the elders there would know already that he had become a "clever" man. For the Ancient Ones had decreed that this was so.

But the Crystal Father had not yet finished, and opening the palm of his hand he showed Kalu that his sacred churinga had not been lost when it had fallen to the ground. With a kind and generous smile the

Crystal Father passed it back to him, assuring him that still more light and magical power would flow forth from it in the days to come.

Finally the Crystal Father told Kalu that from time to time he would also be called upon by members of his camp to summon rain-spirits in the sky. And for this to take place Kalu would need to know how to swing the sacred bull-roarer around his head, wielding it with such magic power that it would create a whirlie-whirlie that would rise up in the sky. So that as a shaman of his people he could enter this magic wind-tunnel and fly skywards in his spirit-vision to meet with the rain-beings in the clouds. These things too he showed him, and then the Crystal Father presented Kalu with the gift of a bull-roarer which bore the sacred emblems of his spirit-country, and which he could use to call the rain when rain was needed by the people.

Now the presence of the Crystal Father began to fade from view, and Kalu found himself once again engulfed in velvet blackness. But he sensed, too, that he was some distance away from the towering rocks, and he felt safer here, with his sacred churinga beside him for protection. And so, marking a circle around him in the red earth, and summoning his guardian spirits to protect him, Kalu lay down to sleep until the coming of the dawn.

As the first pale light of new day came down upon the rock valley, Kalu arose and went back between the towering rocks to retrieve the hunting spears and wooden club which had slipped from his grasp as he had struggled in the dark. Then, once he had found them at the edge of the path, he continued on his way, tracking back toward the stony ridge known as Nallelunga, which he knew was close to home.

Finally he could see his campsite in the distance, and now his eldest boy Jiri was running toward him to welcome him home. Kalu stroked his long fingers through Jiri's curly black hair, gave him a big hug, and told him it was good to be back.

Several seasons passed and still the Spirit Ancestors sent their blessings to Kalu and his people. The hunting had been good, and the seeds and fruits abundant. And everyone knew that Kalu was a "clever" man, for a golden light shone in his eyes and marked him apart.

Now the people of the campsite would come to him for healing, and Kalu would call upon his guardians to bring them back their spirit and make them well. Some had fallen into great sickness and fatigue, for their souls had been snatched away by evil ghosts and taken to rock-holes where they could be hidden beneath the reeds and left to die. And Kalu had gone out looking for these souls in his spirit-vision, and had done battle with the evil ghosts, and had brought their souls safely home.

Sometimes a dark and threatening wind had borne the magic from the evil ones in other lands and places, and this magic had come into their camp at night and had made them crazy, and ill-tempered, and too weak to go out into the land to hunt or dig for food. At those times Kalu would call upon the healing songs which he had been given by the Lizard

Man, whose sacred power and magic could drive these evil forces far away. For with his secret songs Kalu could summon large balls of flickering flame, and these would flare up in the sky and burn to ashes the dark and evil sorcery which had come into their midst.

But then there came a time of great drought, when the red earth was cracked and parched, and fruits and seeds were scarce. This was a time when the rock pools and creeks had all run dry and the animals of the hunt were fewer in number, for there was nothing in the soak for them to drink. The men would go hunting for long days at a time, and would often return with no food at all for the people of the camp. Meanwhile the women who were digging for yams and bush tomatoes would find them withered in the ground. And grubs, too, had become scarce and hard to find.

And as this long season without water brought a growing weariness and discontent among his people, Kalu knew he must now turn to the spirits of the sky, so that rain could once again come to the parched and hungry earth.

Early one morning, as three black crows circled in the western sky, Kalu set off from the man's camp, crossing the empty creek and passing by the white-bark river gums whose leaves were now browned and twisted by the relentless sun. Tracking yet again through the tussock grass and mulga, he came finally to the stony outcrop known as Nallelunga—where he could make his magic and call for the rains to come. This was sacred ground, well known to the guardians of the sky. He would call out to them, and they would know why he had come.

Taking a short knife from his belt, Kalu now slashed his arm and let drops of rich red blood fall upon the ground. Then he took in his hands a cluster of white cockatoo feathers which he had brought with him from the camp, and holding the feathers high above his head he released them to the wind. For he knew that these feathers were like fluffy white clouds, and his drops of red blood were like beads of falling rain. And that together the blood and scattered feathers would make the rains come.

Then Kalu brought forth his sacred bull-roarer and began to whir it strongly in the air, so that soon a thunderous roar engulfed the sky. And a fierce wind arose on Nallelunga, a storm-wind which filled the heavens with dark clouds and made a mighty tunnel rise up into the sky. With his powerful magic Kalu then passed inside this storm-wind tunnel, so he could fly high into the sky and meet with the cloud-spirits who dwelt there. And he would demand of these spirits that they should make healing rains fall upon the red earth.

Away in the camp the people could hear the thunder of Kalu's potent bull-roarer and they could see the grey storm-clouds rising up over Nallelunga. And some could even see Kalu moving about within the clouds, guiding them overhead so the rain would be released and new growth and abundance would come upon the land.

And soon, as Jiri and Tilo looked up from their bark hut at the campsite, they could see that dark storm-clouds had filled the heavens, and soon the rains would come. For Kalu was in the very midst of these clouds, unleashing his mighty sky-magic and directing where the healing rain should fall.

Then there was a mighty roar of thunder, and a deluge of heavy rain fell upon the land. And for a time the red earth became a sodden quagmire, the mulga was turned into swamp, and the bark huts at the campsite were drenched and flooded by the onslaught of the rain. But everyone was happy, for the rain would feed the land and bring the animals and plants back in abundance. Kalu had made his magic with the gods, and they in turn had brought new life back to the earth and had blessed it once again.

With the coming of the rain the season of drought would soon end, for rain fell also in the days ahead. The rock-pools filled and the creeks once again flowed with running water. Emus and rock-wallabies and kangaroos could once again be seen around the soak, scatterings of desert flowers sprang forth from the red earth, and fruits and seeds were once again in plentiful supply.

Meanwhile at the campsite Kalu and Tilo had discussed between themselves that Jiri should now be brought into manhood. This, too, was agreed among the senior Law men, and so a time and place were marked out where Jiri would pass through the first of his initiations and receive teachings from those who knew the Law. And Winjin, who was Kalu's skin-brother and an elder in the group, would come at an agreed time and would take Jiri to a secret place—a place known only to the senior Law men of the camp.

Six days passed, and on the seventh day the sun rose blood-red across the sandhills in the east. And as the sun reached its height in the sky, Winjin came to collect Jiri to take him away into the bushlands—to a secret place where he would be made into a man. Kalu had urged Jiri to remain strong, and had cautioned him too that unless he was asked to speak he should stay silent—even when sharp and savage pain was inflicted upon him. For this too was part of his ordeal, part of his journey in becoming a man. And so Jiri went with Winjin, tracking through the mulga toward the purple mountains in the north— toward the sacred lands of the Lizard Dreaming.

Finally they came to the secret men's place, and here they paused to rest. Then Winjin showed Jiri a sacred marking on the rock—a scar of glistening quartz which had been sent by the sky gods and which had left its mark upon the earth. And Winjin told him also that the Ancestors were all around this place, that they were watching and guiding him at all times, and would be with him in his pain and in his fear.

Now Winjin began to hum softly, and this song was calling forth the lizard-spirits—for they would soon come to this place. Then Winjin daubed Jiri with red ochre, marking out the sacred signs upon his skin so the lizard-spirits would know that Jiri, too, was of their flesh. And now Winjin hummed the song once more, but with greater strength and power than before, and soon Jiri could feel a strange force entering his body, and it was alive with spirits—alive with lizards swimming in his blood and scattering in all directions across his skin.

Now Winjin told Jiri he must remain alone, that he should stay here at the secret men's place until the coming of the new day. And he should be brave and strong, and cast his thought toward the great Earth Mother who had made all things, and to the great Spirit Ancestors who had helped shape the earth. Then, with a rustling of the bushes, Winjin disappeared from view.

Night soon came down upon the secret men's place, shrouding it in silence. Casting around for somewhere to rest, Jiri made a place upon the dusty, uneven ground, shivering in the cold while trying to ease his fears by tracking stars in the night sky. And still his vigil continued. From time to time rustlings and chatterings sounded through the bushes to break the silence, and every now and then the haunting cry of a night owl or dingo would echo though the darkness. This was a lonely and unwelcoming place, and Jiri wondered what lay ahead for him the following day.

At first light three men appeared, but Jiri did not recognize them, for they were heavily daubed in white clay and spoke softly among themselves. Then they gestured that he should lie naked on a smooth rock and look up toward the sky.

In an agonizing moment of sudden pain it was all done. Jiri felt the sharp tearing of his flesh as his foreskin was cut back swiftly by a blade, felt the oozing of his blood as it trickled slowly down his leg. And now they were gauging jagged marks across his chest and cutting with their blades deep into his arms. And they told him he must let his blood flow freely on the earth, for this was the way of the Law.

All this time Jiri had held back from screaming, biting hard on his lip so no squeal of pain or whimpering of weakness would make itself heard. But then glowing, burning sticks were lain in tight formation across his body, and large hot coals rubbed against his skin. And still he held back from showing pain. Still he remained silent.

Then the men told him he should go quickly to a nearby creek, and wash off the burning embers from his skin. And he could rest for a while in the cool water.

When Jiri returned from the creek to take his place within the circle, there were now four men—for Winjin had come back to the secret men's site. He too was daubed with white clay but Jiri recognized his crinkly hair, and his thoughtful, deep-set eyes. And it was Winjin who spoke first.

"You have now become a man," said Winjin, "and now you shall be called Mitamirri—although this name you must keep to yourself. You must not reveal it to any others except those within your skin group, for that is the Law and the Ancestors have decreed that this should be so."

Then, in a lighter tone, he added, "But if you go to work on the cattle station with the whitefellas, you better call yourself Jack—because that is easier to remember, and it won't cause any problems." And with that the men in the circle began to joke and laugh, for they knew that many senior Law men used whitefella names to avoid revealing the secret names given to them by the Dreaming.

Mitamirri laughed too, for the pain of his ordeal was now behind him. But soon the men resumed a more serious mood. And then the talking turned again to the teachings of the Ancestors, and the ways in which the Lizard Spirit had made his journey through this land during the first Dreaming—the Tjukurrpa—when all was new and unformed. And how secret songs had been sung into the earth to make the trees and rock-holes and red sandhills, and how the Lizard Spirit Ancestor had then burrowed into the earth where he remained to this day.

Finally Winjin showed Mitamirri his churinga, with its sacred marks and emblems. "These are the stories of our Dreaming," he said. "This is what binds us all together." Then, opening his hand to reveal a small piece of shining quartz, he said: "This is for you. And you should keep it in a secret place, safe at all times. For it is a sign that you have been made into a man."

One of the other men now rose to his feet and began to swing his bull-roarer in the air. Soon it was moving above them with dizzying speed and as it whirled ever more swiftly it began to speak of what had taken place, and how the spirits were well pleased—for on this day a boy had been made into a man. As a blazing ring of power came down upon the gathered men, it seemed then that thunder had been summoned from the sky—and the Ancient Ones had spoken. And the men felt a deep warmth within their hearts, for the Spirits were among them—and a new member of their group had come to join them in the Dreaming.

So it was that Jiri became a man, and his father knew him from this time onward as Mitamirri, though this name was only whispered privately among those who shared his Dreaming. And later, when he went to work as a cattle-hand on a nearby outstation he was simply known as Jack, and this became his name among those who were not of his spirit-country.

As time passed Kalu showed Mitamirri the sacred Dreaming tracks which meshed in all directions across the ancient land, and he showed him too the sacred lizard-rock where the spirits of the lizards were waiting to be born. And Mitamirri met also with the silver-skinned Lizard Man, and spoke of custodial ways which would bring new life and abundance to the land, and with the spirit-guardians who watched to see its secrets were preserved. For Kalu felt sure that in the seasons ahead Mitamirri would learn more of the ways of the Spirit Ancestors, and would one day become a senior Law man too. Just as Kalu had followed in the footsteps of his father Talpu, so too Mitamirri would also follow in his.

However there came a day when Kalu left the campsite to journey to his sacred lands alone. On this day—with the coming of the dawn—three white cockatoos and three black herons had flown past him in formation as he awoke. And then, beside the entrance of his bark hut, marked out in white feathers upon the red earth, he had seen the most sacred sign from his churinga—a symbol which the Spirit Ancestors themselves had given him, many seasons past. Kalu had quickly swept away these secret markings on the earth in case anyone unfit should cast their eyes upon them and thereby break the Law, but he knew too that this was a special sign. And as he tracked out across the creek, passing the white-bark river gums and heading once again toward Nallelunga, he knew that he was being summoned by forces greater than all the magic and healing he had at his command. That this was magic of the first Dreaming which called him now.

Climbing across the rocky ridge at Nallelunga he headed toward the towering cliffs which rose up high into the sky above the dry creek-bed, and which for Kalu were now linked forever with strange ordeals in the threatening darkness of the night. And now he could see, as he drew closer to the towering cliffs, that the Crystal Father was waiting for him once again.

Even though the sun had risen high up in the sky and Kalu could feel its shimmering heat upon his skin, a much brighter light—a light filled with all the brilliance of dazzling silver quartz—was shining forth from the shadows of the rocky cliff-pass. And now Kalu came once again into the sacred presence of the Crystal Father, and it was he who spoke first.

In words tinged with great sadness, the Crystal Father told Kalu that a song had come forth from the Spirit of the First Dreaming and yet this was not a song of hope and life, but one which spoke instead of dark times coming upon the land—of ill-fortune, sickness and despair being thrust upon the earth. The sacred Dreaming tracks and the songs of the first times would soon be ravaged beyond all bounds by the ways of those who did not know the teachings of the Ancient Ones. For there were many who heeded not the ways of the Spirit Ancestors—who were ravaging the body of the sacred Earth Mother, and tearing her apart. And so now there was a great need—a great and urgent need—for a new and powerful magic, a new and powerful healing, to come upon the land and treat the savage and brutal wounds which had been inflicted upon the Earth Mother. The Great Spirit had called for a worthy and trusted messenger who would come forward from the South—one who could help restore the ancient ways of knowing. And it had been decreed that the Crystal Father would bring this trusted messenger to a sacred place at the very center of the earth—to a place where all Dreaming tracks meet, and where all songs are One Song.

And so it was that the Crystal Father brought his trusted shaman Kalu beyond Nallelunga and the sand-hills of the red earth, beyond the purple mountains of his spirit-country and the custodial lands of the Lizard

Ancestors, to a place known as the Great Lake of Spirit. This was a vast inland sea which Kalu had never seen before, a sea at the very center of the world. And as the Crystal Father explained to Kalu, this sea— which stretched forth in all directions—contained the sacred waters of life itself, for this was the sea from which All Things Come Forth.

Beside this lake Kalu and the Crystal Father would wait until the appointed time, knowing that in other lands, too, the Ancient Ones had also gone in search of loyal and worthy messengers. And from each of the four directions—from North, South, East and West—shamans of the sacred song would come forth as custodians of the Great Spirit, and they would journey to this sacred place.

Now, from the South, Kalu had come. And he would serve as a witness to the rebirth of the world.

EAST

By morning, the rains had departed and a soft, dewy mist had settled over the lake and rice-fields. From the window of her house Teteke watched admiringly as a solitary grey heron strode with quiet dignity through the pale green reeds. Some distance away, a small cluster of tawny ducks preened their feathers and sent rippling patterns scurrying across the surface of the lake.

But Teteke was worried, for her daughter Saimei was sick with a burning fever and had tossed and turned in her bed and called out in pain all through the night. Her soft and gentle face was now flushed and clammy, her eyes wild and haunted. It seemed as if all of her life was draining out of her, draining into nothingness, as her pale and chattering lips called out for warmth and protection. And as Teteke held Saimei's hand to comfort her she knew that this was no ordinary fever, that this was a fever which the gods had ordained.

For Teteke had seen strange shapes darting across Saimei's languid, fevered face—shapes which seemed to twist and writhe, as if ghosts and spirits now dwelt beneath her skin. Then, from time to time, Saimei would become calm, and a deep and rapturous peace would come suddenly upon her, and she would become old and wizened beyond her years—as if time itself had drawn the cycles of its seasons in deep furrows across her brow.

Beside her bed Teteke had placed rice cakes and water and a little jug of sake, but Saimei had shown little appetite for either food or drink. And now she was tossing and turning again—hovering once more between sleep and torment—calling out from time to time that a strange and hostile fire had taken hold inside her. For this was a fire that reached down into the very deepest corners of her soul, a burning, scorching heat which seemed to drain her very essence from within. And yet this was a fire, too, which contained a sense of knowing—as if, by some strange and unfamiliar means, the gods and spirits were speaking to her through its torturing heat.

That night as Saimei fought the ebb and flow of fever coursing through her soul, she had a powerful dream, and in this dream she was flying like a small spirit-bird above her body. And as she looked down upon her slumbering form she watched with horror as she shriveled into a twisted vestige of her former self. Soon only her charred and ashen bones were left behind.

But then as she flew above the shingled rooftop of her small wooden house she could see the lake a short distance away, and she watched with rapt amazement as a haze of muted moonlight played upon the ripples in the water. And already a soft mist had begun to descend.

Then, from within the mist she was surprised to

see the familiar image of her dead father gradually take form—for he had come forth from the shades of the departed ones to speak with her once more.

Kakumei still had long strands of white hair flowing down upon his shoulders, and still he wore his favorite golden robe—the robe he was wearing when he look his leave of earthly life and went to be among the departed ones. But while he had languished with a sickly pallor during his last days, Kakumei now looked vibrant and well, and his eyes spoke of an abiding peace and contentment. And Saimei was overwhelmed with joy at seeing him once more.

Now Kakumei told Saimei in the dream that she had been chosen by the Ancient Ones for tasks which would mark her apart from the world of everyday routines. For she would soon become an ichiko, or shamaness—a spirit-medium through whom the departed ones could speak. And they would pass messages and tidings of good fortune to those whom they had loved while still alive on earth.

Then Kakumei told her also to go to a certain sakaki tree which grew not far from the house, in a grassy, wooded glade beyond the lake. And on this sakaki tree she should drape long strands of blue and white cloth, and also take her mirror there as well. And as she looked into her mirror she would see a kami, or spirit, that had come down from the mountain to live within the tree, and this kami would become her spirit-guardian. This kami would then be with her always, and would come to her when needed—whether in dreams or in the clear light of day—and would show her the pathways to the spirit-world.

Kakumei told her also that her fever would pass, that the fierce heat of her sickness would soon leave her body. And as she gradually regained her health she would begin to see the world in ways not revealed to others. Then, as Kakumei prepared to return once more to the land of the departed ones, he told Saimei he would leave a sign that this was a true dream, a dream she could believe in, and which would stay with her always. And when the time came for Saimei to awake next day, she would find a small silver dagger on her pillow, and she would know that this had come as a gift from her father in the spirit-world.

Later, as the mist began to rise up from the lake and the light of new morning sent flickering patterns through the bamboo blinds drawn across her window, Saimei awoke from her fever and felt already that the strong fires which had raged within her soul had now begun to ease. Then, reaching across her pillow, she found the small silver dagger which Kakumei had promised he would leave for her.

Saimei called out to her mother, and Teteke came quickly to her side, placing her hand upon her daughter's clammy brow. And she could see that already the tides of sickness had begun to subside, and that a new strength was growing in Saimei and she would soon be well once more.

Saimei then told her mother about her dream, how she had flown like a small spirit-bird above her burning body, and how she had spoken with her beloved father, Kakumei—who had come to meet with her from the world of the departed ones. He had told her she would soon become a shamaness—a medium of the spirit world. And he had promised to leave a small silver dagger resting on her pillow to show that this was indeed a true dream. Teteke listened in amazement to all these things and then, nestling the small silver dagger within the palm of her hand—a gift from her long-departed husband—she knew beyond doubt that the gods had spoken through this dream. That her daughter had indeed been set apart to be a medium for the spirits, and a messenger for the Ancient Ones.

A few days passed, and gradually Saimei regained her strength. And then, when she was well, she went late one afternoon to the leafy glade beyond the lake. There—upon the sakaki tree—she draped strands of blue and white cloth, as she had been told. And looking intently in her small mirror, she called for a kami to come forth from the tree and become her spirit-guardian.

For a few moments there was only silence. But then vivid patterns of bright light filled her mirror and she was dazzled by its shimmering radiance. And Saimei saw that a beautiful kingfisher—whose feathers glistened green and azure blue—had come to meet her from the sakaki tree.

Gazing deep into its shining, golden eyes Saimei knew that this was no ordinary bird that lived beside the lake. An ancient soul dwelt within this creature—a kami from the highest and most sacred spheres of all, one which had come down from the heavens beyond the snowy peaks of Mount Ikuta. And seeing that Saimei was well versed in the ways of the spirit, the kingfisher spoke to her now in words which she would understand.

"I am known as Nifu," said the azure kingfisher, "and I guard the sacred waters which flow down from Mount Ikuta, and which fill all the lakes and rivers and bring new life and abundance to the rice fields. And I know the secret pathways which entwine the sacred mountain—paths which twist and turn and which lead high up through the pine trees, even to the very peak itself. Where one day you too may meet the Goddess of the Waters. And although you may not always glimpse me by your side, I will be with you always as your guardian."

Saimei felt deeply moved by Nifu's words of kindness and promised then to build a small stone shrine beneath the sacred sakaki tree where she would honor Nifu and the Goddess of the Waters with gifts of rice and dried fish, as well as offerings of fruit and wild flowers. And Nifu told her too that she must help her mother with her daily observances, just as her cousin Sujin worked tirelessly in the rice fields, and that soon the time would come when she would be shown new pathways in the world of spirit. For then she would become known within her village as one who could move freely between the living and the dead—one who could heal those whose souls had been snatched away by dark and vengeful spirits and taken to the underworld.

From this time onward Saimei took special care to help her mother with her daily observances, and she would often travel with her to the shrines at the foot of Mount Ikuta, where together they would place flowers and food as gifts for the gods and spirits of the land. And her mother explained that with the coming of Spring—as the first flowers showed their petals through the last drifts of snow—the great kami-spirits of the sacred mountain would come down from the wooded slopes and then would dwell within the fields and nearby lake, for there they could see the planting of the rice and watch over the crop until the time of harvest. Then, in the fading days of autumn, the kami-spirits would once again take their leave, and return to the sacred mountain whence they came.

Teteke also took Saimei upon a narrow track lined with ferns and wild flowers—a track which wound its way through many twists and turns at the foot of Mount Ikuta. And here, beneath this great and sacred mountain, they came to a place where berries and grasses grew in rich abundance beside a fast-flowing stream, and where a single silver birch tree reached high into the sky. This tree Teteke had chosen as one to honor Kakumei, and here she had built a small mound of grey stones. With each full moon she would come to this silver birch and place a new stone upon the mound—for this was her way of honoring his memory, among all departed ones.

And there were special markings which had been cut upon the tree—little notches incised upon its mottled, weathered bark—and these were the steps which led up into the heavens.

Teteke told Saimei how in the month of the seventh moon large fires would be lit at night upon the mountain-tops and hills, and bright lanterns placed beside the lake. And these fires would light a path for the spirits of the Ancient Ones and long departed souls, who could then find their way down the wooded slopes to be among their loved ones once again. One evening, during the lighting of the fires, Teteke had seen the spirit of her great-grandmother floating above the lake, and at this time, too, the spirits of her father and sister had come inside the house to dwell beside the hearth. And often in the seventh month clusters of dappled dragonflies would also come, and they would hover in the air and fly around the people in the village. For they too were spirits of the dead, and the people knew not to harm or catch them, and instead took great care to honor them and call out to them with greetings—for they were pleased that the long departed ones had come back among them once again.

Then, one day, word came that Yutaki—a well known shamaness—was coming to the village from a region in the north. Yutaki was famed among her people for her chanting, and for her haunting, uplifting songs. And she knew how to journey to the underworld in her spirit-vision, retrieving souls snatched away by harmful spirits and evil sorcerers. For she had sojourned among the shaman women who lived upon the Ryukyu islands, and she had learned their gifts of prophecy and their ways of speaking with the dead. And with this knowledge Yutaki would travel from village to village, and she would be called on by those who sought her skills of healing or who wished her to speak with spirits, ghosts or ancestors, on their behalf.

And so Teteke sent word that she would like to meet with Yutaki, and tell her of her daughter's dreams and visions. How Saimei had been seized with fever, how her soul had flown above her body like a spirit-bird, and how her long-departed father Kakumei had told her she would soon become an ichiko, or shamaness, among the people of her village. These were the things Teteke wished to tell, and she felt sure that Yutaki would understand.

Clothed in robes of burnished silk, Yutaki rode upon a white horse and traveled alone, bringing with her the tools of sacred magic for which she was renowned. And the people of the villages would feed her and give her gifts and see that she was well looked after in their homes. For Yutaki knew the ways of the shaman-women, and she was greatly honored and respected wherever she went.

Yutaki had in her possession a fine catalpa bow, carved from elm-wood and inlaid with magic emblems and motifs—and this bow had been given to her by the sibyls of the Ryukyu islands. Yutaki knew how to play upon this bow with a bamboo rod, and at the same time she would sing sacred songs in her fine, pure voice—a voice so pure that some said it was like the nectar from a flower.

Yutaki also had a leather drum, and she would beat upon this drum with a small wooden stick. This was a drum of great power and resonance and, as her drumming gathered strength, the voices of the departed ones would echo like a chorus from its rim. And then Yutaki's soul would rise up like a bird, soaring free above the highest pines and birches. So that through the power of her drum and her sacred songs she would travel in her spirit-vision and come before the great Goddess and the spirits in her realm.

Then the morning arrived when Yutaki agreed to meet with Teteke and Saimei in their home. Leaving her white horse tethered at the gate, Yutaki walked up the stony path to the front porch, bringing with her the small leather drum and her catalpa bow. And Teteke was greatly pleased that Yutaki had come to visit, for she knew she would look deep within her daughter's soul and see the ways which lay ahead. And after gifts had been given and sweet tea offered to their guest, Teteke called Saimei to her side, so she could meet with Yutaki, and a plan could then be made.

For a while Saimei sat in silence, waiting for Yutaki to speak first—out of respect for this famed and honored healer who had come to their village. And all this time Yutaki, too, was watching and observing—waiting for the spirits to show their signs. Yutaki could see that ghosts and spirits had come to be with Saimei, that they had found their home deep within her soul. Yutaki could also see that an azure light glowed upon her brow—and this was the light of Nifu, who had brought protection to her path. The spirit of Kakumei was with her too, and dwelt within her heart. And there would be others to come—for with the calling of the guardians Saimei would learn to move ever more certainly on her path between the worlds.

Finally Saimei and Yutaki spoke of how they might proceed, how Saimei could, with time, become a shamaness for her people. And Yutaki spoke then of certain tasks and obligations, and told her that these must be performed with diligence and care, and great respect, in order to aid the purpose which lay ahead.

And this is what she told her: that in the early hours of morning Saimei should make her way to a swiftly moving stream—a stream whose currents flowed down from the highest peaks of Mount Ikuta—and there she must bathe within its cold, unsullied waters to become pure within her being. And this she should perform, day after day, until the coming of the next full moon. And there were certain secret songs which Yutaki would teach her, and these she should sing to bring power to her soul. She should sojourn too upon the slopes of Mount Ikuta, among the pines and silver birches, so the spirits of the mountain would come to know her presence, and would welcome her there. And in her sojourn on the mountain she should fast for seven days, and then—after her fasting—she should partake only of nuts and berries, and should forgo the rice and meat and beans that she had eaten until now.

Then, when these things had been done, Yutaki would return to Saimei's village, and rituals would be performed and sacreds songs sung, so that

Saimei would become a shamaness and a healer for her people.

So it came to pass that Saimei made her way once more to Mount Ikuta and found the place where she had come with her mother—where berries and grasses and wild flowers grew in rich abundance. Here—in the sacred stream which had swept down from the mountain—she bathed each morning, immersing her body in its icy waters in order to become pure within herself. For Yutaki had told her if she did this the spirits would be well pleased, and they in turn would flow like a stream through every corner of her soul.

With the passing of each day, Saimei ventured still further upon the hidden tracks and pathways which entwined the sacred mountain—upon paths which turned and twisted in all directions through the pines and silver birches. And always Nifu would be with her, lighting her path and darting swiftly from one side to another. For he knew he must show her the secret places within the forest where she could come in safety to seek the counsel of her soul.

When Saimei had done what had been asked of her—when she had bathed and fasted and sojourned on the mountain—word was sent to Yutaki asking her to come back to the village, for Saimei and her mother were ready to receive her. And so she returned upon her white horse, with her implements of magic and healing, and she could see that a pure spirit moved in Saimei's soul and she was ready to become a shamaness.

The soft warmth of summer was now upon them and the pure mountain waters had brought life and abundance to the rice fields. On the lake beside Saimei's house a small cluster of tawny ducks continued their routines, preening their feathers and sending rippling patterns scurrying across the surface of the water. And still, from time to time, a solitary grey heron could be seen—striding majestically through the green reeds.

Once again Yutaki had brought her drum and her fine catalpa bow—and she had also brought with her some brightly tufted arrows which she would fire into the sky to let the gods and spirits know her ritual had begun. Yutaki and Saimei set aside the fifth evening of the fifth month because they knew that at this time the kami-spirits from Mount Ikuta had already come down from the wooded slopes to dwell within the rice fields and the lake—and here they would watch the sacred ritual from their place between the worlds.

And so on the fifth evening of the fifth month a small group of family and friends gathered at Saimei's house beside the lake, and red lanterns were lit so that the spirits could watch from afar. And Yutaki and Saimei prayed and sang and chanted, and a powerful healing came down upon them—a blessing from the gods on Mount Ikuta.

While Yutaki was adorned in long and flowing robes whose colors were of the dusk and darkening sky, Saimei wore a dress of pure white silk which some thought looked like drifts of winter snow. But Saimei knew it as a ritual dress of death, a dress she must wear as she died before the world and then was born anew. For Yutaki would call a new spirit to come and dwell within her, and this spirit would then fill her soul with new life and hope.

Now as the soft light of evening sent purple shadows dancing across the lake, everyone gathered beside the house to watch as Yutaki fired her tufted arrows high into the air, and called for a healing spirit to come down into their midst. For as Yutaki had foretold, this spirit would dwell in Saimei's soul, and would give guidance and wise counsel in the times which lay ahead.

Then Yutaki began to play upon the string of her catalpa bow, and her chants and spirit-songs took flight into the air. And as Saimei sat motionless before her teacher, her hands began to tremble and her body began to shake, and already a powerful spirit had begun to stir within her soul. Then Yutaki asked aloud which god or spirit had come here in their midst. And soon Saimei's pale and trembling lips spoke the words which all had come to hear, and all who had gathered there by the lake knew then that the Goddess of the Waters had come among them, and she had chosen Saimei as a vessel for her gifts.

But now Saimei fell down in a faint upon the ground, and it seemed suddenly that her life had drained away. And some feared her soul had been captured by the spirits and taken to other realms—for her arms and legs lay limp and lifeless at her side, and a white and ghostly pallor had now come upon her face. But swiftly she was carried to her room, and sweet-smelling herbs cast upon her cheek. And her mother helped undress her so she could discard the dress of death, and wear another gown instead. And its color would speak of life instead of death, and it would show all who had gathered there that a new strength and purpose had come into her soul.

Soon Saimei revived, her breath uplifted by the scent of sweet herbs. And again she came before those who had gathered at the lake—this time in a gown of purest blue, as pure as the sacred waters which flowed on Mount Ikuta. For, as Yutaki explained, Saimei's ritual marked a change within her soul, and she had passed from one life to another. And it was clear to everyone that new life had returned to her, bringing color to her pale lips—and soon a blush of pink appeared upon her cheeks. Her eyes were bright and clear, and a new light shone from them. And everyone knew that Saimei had returned to live among them—as a shamaness and healer.

Now Saimei sat upright on the ground, her hands outstretched before her, her palms uplifted to the sky—as she offered a prayer of welcoming acceptance to the Goddess of the Waters. And as the prayer came to a close, a shimmering haze of light arose within their midst, for the Goddess was among them, and a spirit of cleansing and renewal came down upon those who had gathered at the lake. And some sensed too that Kakumei stood beside his daughter, and that Nifu was with her also. And Saimei gave thanks to Yutaki for coming to the village, and for sharing her healing gifts with those who had sought her blessings.

Then in joy and celebration small jugs of sake were passed among the guests and a feast was held, with fine foods and exotic fruits and sweet tea shared among those who had gathered at the lake. And the guests offered praises to the Goddess of the Waters—and to the kami-spirits who had come down into the rice fields from the slopes of Mount Ikuta. For the people of the village knew the gods still watched over them, and shared in their happiness and hope.

With the departure of Yutaki, Saimei now felt a deep need to journey still further upon the paths of the Ancient Ones. Late one afternoon, as the sun was dipping low across the rice fields, she went again to the leafy glade beyond the lake and sat upon the grass before her sacred sakaki tree. And now, as she rested with her eyes closed and her heart open, she asked for Nifu to appear.

Then within her spirit-vision the sakaki tree began to quiver and waver, as if seized by a strong spirit-wind. Suddenly it became much larger, towering above her so its leafy branches reached out to fill the sky—its trunk pointing high up to the heavens. And the tree was bathed in green and golden light, as if a wondrous haze of sun-dew had poured across its leaves.

Again Nifu was here, resplendent in his green and azure blue, but this time he did not speak—and turning toward the tree he now gestured to Saimei that she should follow him. And soon they were flying together—flying from branch to branch—and the sakaki tree had become a world unto itself.

From time to time Saimei noticed little birds and animals that lived within the branches, and she also saw a golden snake that had entwined itself around the outer limbs. And these creatures she knew to be other kami-spirits who had come here from the mountain, for they too had made this tree their home.

But then, just as rapidly as it had grown and filled the sky, the sakaki tree vanished from view, and suddenly Saimei saw that Nifu was no longer with her, and she was travelling alone—moving through the darkening sky toward stars which lit the heavens. And as she drew closer to the stars she saw that they had formed a pathway for her journey—a row of glistening torches that danced with silver light as she made her way forward. And the path was calling her onward—calling her to come among the spirits and departed ones—and she knew it was her mission to go among these spirits, for this had been decreed and she was now a vessel for the gods.

Now as Saimei sped swiftly through the sky she could see rising ahead of her a tall bridge whose beams and arches shone with silver light—and this was a bridge which spanned the gulf between the worlds, the gulf between the living and the dead.

Saimei saw too that a robed figure stood beside the bridge. And soon she could see that this was none other than the Goddess of the Waters—for the Goddess had come to meet her beside the bridge of light.

The Goddess stood resplendent in robes of flowing blue and silver, and her hair was glistening with the dew of early sunrise. For this was the Goddess whose very being spoke of hope and renewal, whose sacred waters flowed down from Mount Ikuta to feed the land. And there in the night sky her jeweled body sparkled like drops of crystal rain, and her healing song was the gift of life itself.

And as Saimei approached the Goddess of the Waters she bowed her head respectfully and kept her silence, for she knew that among all the gods and goddesses she alone could touch the furthest reaches of her soul.

And soon Saimei felt herself being filled with graceful, flowing music, and the Goddess was pouring into her a knowledge of both the heavens and the lower worlds which lay beneath the earth. And as she stood there beside the sacred bridge of light, it was as if she had traversed these distant realms in the twinkling of an eye.

For a time Saimei floated freely among the kamis of the sky and she loved them, for these were gentle spirits—like the mist which comes in with the dawn. But then, in an instant, she came among forsaken spirits of the dead—those whose souls were languishing in dark worlds beneath the earth, in misery and sickness, and in states of degradation. And these were human souls whose lives had been snatched away by mischievous and malevolent forces.

And Saimei knew too that she could journey to the heavens and the world beneath the earth—and she could do this by flying in spirit through the roots and branches of a vast and noble tree: her sakaki tree. For this tree was like a ladder between the worlds, a ladder of the spirit whose highest branches reached far up to the heavens, just as its tangled roots reached down into the murky worlds below. And, as a healer for her people she knew that she must journey far and wide upon this tree—to worlds above and worlds below—and she would be called upon to bring life and spirit to the people most in need.

When this lesson had been shown to her, the Goddess of the Waters told Saimei she could now make her way across the sacred bridge of light. But this was a special gesture, given only to a few. For without the blessing of the gods and goddesses the souls of living beings were not allowed to cross this bridge and then return from whence they came. Only those who had passed through death itself—the spirits of departed ones—could journey across the bridge and pass freely from one world to another.

So, with the blessing of the Goddess of the Waters, Saimei now made her way across the sacred bridge of light. And as she reached the other side she could see a familiar figure coming to meet her from the shades beyond the bridge. This was her beloved father, Kakumei.

Kakumei appeared as he had before, for he lived now in a world beyond time and change and aging—and ever this would be so. Long strands of white hair flowed down upon his shoulders, and still he wore his favorite golden robe—the robe he was wearing when he took his leave of earthly life and went to be among the departed ones. And his eyes spoke still of an abiding sense of peace.

Again Saimei recalled her fever, and her powerful dream from earlier times when she had flown like a spirit-bird in the sky. And her father had told her that soon she would become a shamaness and healer, and later he had watched proudly as Yutaki called a spirit into her—the Goddess of the Waters. And she knew that, like Nifu, he would be with her always.

Kakumei could see already that Saimei had ventured on the inner paths of spirit—that the Goddess of the Waters had poured this knowing into her, and that now she knew the vast terrain of the higher and lower worlds. That as a shamaness and healer she would come to these places to find the souls of those who were sick and dispirited—and would then take their souls back with her to the world of the living, that they might become well again.

But Kakumei knew too that healers in all lands and places were in need of certain allies, that guardians and spirit-helpers must be summoned to assist upon the pathways of the spirit. And while Nifu had come to be with Saimei as her kami and her guardian, she would also be in need of other spirit-helpers in the times which lay ahead. And so Kakumei had brought with him a spirit-being which he would offer to her now—a creature of great knowing and foresight that could guide her on the hidden and secret paths. And Kakumei asked Saimei to cast her gaze within the misty shades around her, and this creature would then present itself before her, as an ally and a friend.

Now, from within a haze of muted light the spirit-guardian came forward—and Saimei saw that it was a small, agile fox. Its fur was of deep russet red, its face of purest white. And sharp brown eyes looked back at her, the eyes of a guardian who knew the secret ways. And Saimei knew well that foxes were renowned for their foresight and their knowledge—that many shamanesses throughout the land had taken foxes as their spirit-helpers for they could seek out secret places, and go in search of lost or forgotten things. And spirit-foxes could pass unseen between the worlds to bring the healer to hidden places which would not otherwise be found.

And so Saimei accepted this spirit-creature from her father with great thanks and appreciation, and promised to feed it with bean curd and other tasty morsels to which it had become accustomed. And Kakumei gave her also a small golden bell and said that whenever this bell was rung the red fox would appear by her side. The fox's name was Miko—which means one who has become the eyes and voice of the ancestral spirits.

Now, once again, Kakumei said he must take his leave and Saimei should return once more to the world of the living. And so she travelled back across the bridge of light, back through the night sky along the path of silver torches, and came finally to her sacred sakaki tree. And now she descended through its leafy branches until she came finally to the base of its trunk and found herself once more in the glade beyond the lake. And in her hand she held the small golden bell which she could use to call her new spirit-helper. It would remain hidden in a special place which only she knew, and like the small silver dagger which she had been given earlier, it would represent a special bond with her father, a gift from the realm of the departed ones.

Saimei now devoted her days to her work as a healer in the village. She possessed her own drum and bow—for these Yutaki had given her—and she would go from house to house, and to other neighborhoods near by, to heed the calls of those who had been stricken with sudden sickness and misfortune. Sometimes, too, she would be asked to become a vessel for the ancestors, and at these times she would become still, and journey deep within herself, and become open so the gods and spirits could find their voice and speak through her. And for these services the people would reward her with gifts of food and clothing, and sweet smelling herbs.

Saimei now knew the sacred songs, and she would pound her drum and play upon the string of her catalpa bow. Then her soul would rise up, and she would journey upon the branches of her sakaki tree. And there she would meet Nifu, or call Miko with her golden bell. Together they would venture in far-off realms to find spirits that had been hidden or snatched away, and then they would bring them back among the living, and Saimei would sing her healing songs and breathe their souls back inside their bodies—so that the spirit of well-being would come among them once again.

Still Saimei took special care to help her mother with her daily observances, and still she would travel with her to the shrines at the foot of Mount Ikuta, where together they would place flowers and food as gifts for the gods and spirits of the land. And together they would also travel to the place beneath the mountain where berries and grasses grew in rich abundance, and where a single silver birch tree reached high into the sky. For this was the tree which Teteke had chosen as one to honor Kakumei, and where she had built a small mound of grey stones. Now with each full moon Saimei would come with her mother to visit this silver birch, and she too would place a new stone upon the mound—for this had also become her way of honoring his memory. And she knew that deep within her heart Kakumei was with her always, and watched over her from his home beyond the bridge of light.

Then one morning toward the end of summer, and before the hour of sunrise, Saimei looked out from her window and she could see that once again a soft mist had come down upon the lake. And now as she watched, a silver bridge of light took shape above the lake, and this was a place where one could cross between the worlds.

Now Kakumei was coming across the bridge in his golden robes, and soon he had crossed the bridge and was walking slowly toward the house. And then as Saimei looked out toward the entrance of her house she could see that he had come to welcome Teteke to the world of spirit, and Teteke had joined him now, and once again they were united. Together, hand in hand, they walked back across the sacred bridge of light, and then they were lost within the soft mist, and had vanished out of view.

Then, when Saimei went over to her mother's room she found her aged and wrinkled body lying in quiet and peaceful repose upon her bed. And Saimei knew that her spirit had departed, that she had now gone to dwell with Kakumei in the world beyond the shades.

Silently, and with mixed feelings of joy and sadness, Saimei placed a cluster of small wildflowers above her mother's heart. And she knew that although her mother was now lost to this world, she still lived and breathed within another—that now she would dwell in a place beyond time and change and aging.

So it came to pass that Teteke departed from the land of the living and Saimei would have to dwell alone, in her small house beside the rice-fields and the lake.

In the middle of the seventh month, the festival of Bon came once again to Saimei's village—and large fires were lit at night upon the mountain-tops and hills, and bright lanterns were placed beside the lake. For it was said that these fires would light a path for the spirits of the Ancient Ones and long departed souls, who could then find their way down the wooded slopes to be among their loved ones once again. And Saimei hoped within her heart that Kakumei and Teteke would come to visit her, and that they would stay within the house and find a place beside the hearth.

So she made offerings of food and sweet incense, and filled the house with wild flowers—flowers whose rich scent would serve to welcome them if indeed they chose to come. And by night she would send forth her prayers, urging her parents to visit during the festival of Bon.

As the festival began, towering fires were lit upon the hilltops and in the dusky light of evening the bright red lanterns sent their flickering reflections dancing across the lake. And Saimei sat down upon the grass in quiet reflection, to ponder on these things.

Then to her great delight, as she looked out across the lake, the silver bridge of light took shape once again above the rippling waters. And Saimei watched with pleasure as her father and mother came toward her, hand in hand. There too was Nifu—his azure feathers glistening in the light. And Miko was with them also, his piercing eyes alert and ever watchful as he made his way beside them on the bridge.

But Saimei could see now that they had not come in celebration, and that another task or purpose had brought them here tonight. For there was tension in their faces, and scarcely time for greetings and good wishes.

Then, pausing by the lake, Kakumei called out to Saimei that she must join them with great haste, for the Goddess of the Waters had asked them all to come. They must make their way swiftly to the foot of Mount Ikuta, and there the Goddess would appear before them. And she would counsel them further on matters of great import.

So it came to pass that as evening came down around them, Kakumei and Teteke and Saimei, together with their guardians, set out along the stony track which led out of the village toward the sacred mountain. Miko moved on ahead so that they would come quickly to Mount Ikuta, and Nifu's azure light was like a beacon for their path.

They made their way speedily through dense pines and mottled silver birches until they came finally to the place where berries and grasses grew in rich abundance beside the fast-flowing stream, and where a single silver birch tree reached high into the sky. And here beside the small mound of grey stones which had been built to honor Kakumei, the Goddess of the Waters awaited them.

A soft light now adorned the grasses and the trees as if they wore a shroud of silver mist. And as

Kakumei, Teteke and Saimei took their place before
the Goddess, a song of great and timeless beauty rose
up from deep within the earth. Its music told a story
which had been with them always—for it spoke of
the sacred waters of Mount Ikuta, and how these
waters gave the gift of never-ending life.

Once again the Goddess was awesome to behold,
her fine robes flowing in folds of resplendent blue and
silver, her jeweled body sparkling like drops of crystal
rain. But now there was a deep sadness in her eyes,
and a deep grief had taken hold within her heart.

She told them now why they had been summoned to this place—that there was now a great and
urgent need to reaffirm the pure and holy presence
of Mount Ikuta—to honor and preserve it for all the
times ahead. For as the people had always known,
this great and noble mountain had been a source of
sacred life through all the seasons past, and the waters
from the mountain had flown down into the streams,
and would forever bring new life to the foothills and
the rice-fields down below. And the kami-spirits had
come down from the sky and had come to dwell

here on the mountain, in this blessed and sanctified place. This had been affirmed in the stories of the people, and this had always been so—from earliest times till now.

But sad and unhappy ways had come upon the earth and things must be made right again. And it had been decreed that one with pure and true intent—one who knew the ways of spirit—should come to Mount Ikuta. This chosen person would be a true servant of the Ancient Ones and would henceforth be their messenger, and would journey with the Goddess to a secret and holy place. And this was a place which had been kept sacred by the Ancient Ones since the creation of the world.

Hearing these things, Saimei now stepped forward to present herself as a servant of the Ancient Ones— for she would be greatly honored to follow in the footsteps of the Goddess, and would do her bidding as required. And Kakumei and Teteke, too, affirmed that the Goddess must take their daughter Saimei, for her intent was pure and trustworthy, and she would surely serve as a vessel for the spirit.

Now, as Kakumei, Teteke and Saimei looked up toward the sky, the Goddess of the Waters held her hands up high toward the peak of Mount Ikuta. And as they watched, dark clouds gathered above the mountain and a bolt of silver lightning struck the very peak itself, and rippled down through the densely wooded slopes. And a large doorway opened in the earth.

As they looked inside the doorway they could see that the mountain itself was lit from within by a brilliant, glowing orb—like a sun that glowed within—and that its light revealed a narrow rocky path which led down into the earth. Then the Goddess of the Waters called Saimei to her side, and together they passed through the open doorway to begin their journey—down into the depths. And as the door closed slowly behind them, darkness fell upon the land once more, and it was left to Kakumei and Teteke and the guardian spirits to return from whence they came.

Meanwhile Saimei and the Goddess of the Waters continued their descent beneath the sacred mountain, for they were journeying now toward a deep and holy place within the earth. And after they had passed through hidden caves and passages far beneath the mountain, they came finally to a place of great sanctity and purity—a place which lay beyond the realm of spirits and beyond the bridge of light.

It was in this way that the Goddess of the Waters brought Saimei to the Great Lake of Spirit, a vast inland sea which lay deep beneath Mount Ikuta at the very center of the world. And as they paused to rest, the Goddess explained to Saimei that this vast eternal sea—a sea which had existed before the world was formed—contained the sacred waters of life itself, even those waters which flowed forth upon the slopes of Mount Ikuta. For this was the sacred sea from which All Things Come Forth.

Now Saimei and the Goddess of the Waters would wait until the appointed time, knowing that in other lands, too, the Ancient Ones had also gone in search of loyal and worthy messengers. For it had been decreed that from each of the four directions—from North, South, East and West—shamans and healers of the sacred song would come forth as custodians of the Great Spirit, and they would then journey to this sacred place.

And the gods were well pleased that, from the East, Saimei had come. For she too would serve as a witness to the rebirth of the world.

WEST

Soon the sun would pass behind the mountains and then the uneasy light of dusk would fall upon the forest. As Baiya looked out into the dense foliage around the clearing he could hear the eerie songs of the night birds as they gathered in the branches. Their shrill, high-pitched chanting always sent a shiver down his spine, for it was at dusk that the spirits of those who had recently died would roam among the living, visiting their former abodes one last time before wandering off into the depths of the forest. This was a time to remain strong within oneself, strong within one's soul.

But tonight, once again, there would be a gathering in the long-house and the men would come together in friendship, their faces painted with the sacred signs and markings that had been given to them by their ancestors. They would bring with them their rattles and their beating sticks. Then great myths and stories would be told, and the sacred songs sung. And the men would drink in turn from the gourd—drink the potion which they had always drunk since times past, to open their hearts to the ways of the spirits and to the many paths of vision.

As night came down upon the forest, Baiya made his way across the clearing to the rocky track which led up to the long-house. Away in the distance he could hear his dogs barking and the sound of chickens scratching in the earth. Within the depths of the forest the never-ending chirping of the night birds and the insects would continue until dawn.

His face and arms were freshly painted with the special markings that were sacred to his people, and he had brought with him his rattles and his feather headband, and a gourd of sweet manioc beer to drink later in the evening. As he passed by the corn field and the cleared land beside the forest he could see that the other men were now arriving as well. A torch had been lit inside and a small patch of reddish light shone forth from the entrance to the long-house, blending with the intense darkness of the night.

Some of the men had already taken their places upon the small wooden stools around the hearth. And there, amidst the flickering light and shadows of the long-house, it was as if fragments of a rainbow had come down within their midst, for each of the men wore a headband of brightly colored toucan feathers and their olive-brown skins were glistening with vivid lines and motifs. Baiya's friend, Setuma, had brought the sacred jug of yajé and wore decorative seed rattles upon his elbows and his ankles. And already Waka was playing a tune upon his flute.

As Baiya entered the long-house the other men turned to greet him. He was the senior man among them, and it was he who would have the task of passing the sacred bowls of yajé from person to person around the room.

Soon they began to talk among themselves about their encounters with the spirits, and about special cures and spells. Some spoke too about the bewitching magic that had come in from the neighboring people who lived lower down the mountains.

Now Setuma placed the pot of yajé in the center of the room where the torch had been lit, and soon it was time for Baiya to pass the potion around. Stirring the liquid with a wooden stick, Baiya then poured it into two gourd vessels. And as these were passed from one man to the next, Waka began to play again upon his flute while Forako hummed and sang.

Then they knew that the Ancient Ones and spirits had come among them in the long-house, for they began to shake and tremble, and soon they were caught up in a swirling torrent which threatened to subsume them, like an omen from the gods. And now a shimmering haze filled the long-house and a dazzling array of colors came down around them, and they swam within these colors as if in a glistening mountain stream. And as the wooden posts within the long-house transformed into richly jewelled snakes that writhed and twisted and climbed up into the rafters, a shrill wailing of spirit-voices chorused through the air.

Soon the men were dancing together in the center of the long-house—their seed bracelets chattering like buzzing insects, their brightly colored headbands darting like little birds around the room. They had begun to sing among themselves as well—songs which had first come to them from deep within the earth or which had fallen from the air in a fine gossamer mist, filling them with peace. And now there was no fear of evil magic, no threat of warring neighbors, no feeling of bewitchment. For they were dancing the dance of the humming bird spirits, and singing the story of the honey bees, and offering tributes to the spirit of the yellow jaguar with its fierce eyes, who was now a protector and a friend.

Later in the night, when the reveling was over and the story-telling complete, Baiya walked back slowly to his palm-thatch house at the edge of the forest. For a time he stood in silence near the narrow mountain stream, and here he listened to the welcome croaking of the frogs and toads, and to the gentle lapping of the water as it flowed across the stones. And here he reflected on how he himself had become a shaman and a healer.

Above him in the night sky the stars glistened from all directions like little silver torches. Baiya recalled that the Ancient Ones themselves had once come from the stars—that the Star-people had walked upon the earth with the coming of the first dawn. For it was they who had brought the sacred yajé to the earth and had then shown the ancestors how to use it to meet the spirits.

It was his teacher, Felisario, who had first told him about these things—Felisario, the master shaman, who had guided him upon the spirit path when he was still only a youth.

Baiya had had dreams of the spirit creatures for as long as he could remember, and they would come to him, night after night, whispering in his ears and singing to him from the depths of his soul. He would wake in a cold sweat after meeting with glint-eyed jaguars and dreaming of giant anacondas writhing at the foot of his bed. Later he would speak privately of these things with his older brother, Maleiwa, and he would ask him if, some time in the future, he would become a shaman—a master of the spirit animals.

Then one day, as the visions continued, Maleiwa told him he should visit Felisario—a respected and trusted shaman who lived in a small palm-thatch house in the very heart of the forest. Maleiwa told him that Felisario would know very soon if he had the making of a shaman, for he would explore the mysterious, radiant light which shone forth from the living soul, and which only a shaman could see. And here he would look for the sacred signs and colors which had been placed there by the gods, and then he would know if Baiya's quest was pure and true, and whether a healing power was written in his heart.

And so, soon after his eighteenth birthday, Baiya made his way across the rocky ridge close by Xini Falls and tracked through densely layered forest undergrowth to a small clearing at the foot of the mountain. And then he came finally to the palm-thatch house where Felisario lived alone, with his chickens and his dogs and his weed-infested garden.

Felisario was working with his crops and looked up unconcerned as Baiya approached, for he knew that this was no enemy who had ventured on his land. And, for his part, Baiya was humble and reserved, fully aware that he had come into the presence of one skilled in the ways of magic and the spirits.

Felisario had a wide and open face, and few lines marked his brow. A distinctive light shone forth from his deep brown eyes, a light which Maleiwa had told him to watch out for as the mark of a true shaman. There was a calm strength in Felisario—a sense of great poise and balance—and there was warmth and kindness too, for Felisario could tell why he had come.

Baiya offered gifts of food and tobacco and told Felisario he wished to learn the ways of healing. And by way of repayment, he would be pleased to tend the shaman's crops, and prepare his manioc beer, and weed his garden, and care for his patch of maize…and anything else he wished.

Felisario offered no immediate response but instead gestured for Baiya to remove his shirt and lie prostrate upon the ground. And now Felisario could see that Baiya's chest thronged with little particles of light, and that these aligned themselves in sacred shapes and patterns. He was pleased to see this in the body of one so young, for the spirits themselves had made these signs, and in Baiya they were pure and true.

Felisario had no son of his own with whom to share his knowledge, and it seemed now that the spirits had brought them together. And so the path was made open for Baiya to become an apprentice to Felisario, and a small bed of matted palm leaves was prepared at one end of the house. Baiya would have to learn to subsist on smoked meat, manioc and mashed fruit, although there would be bush-partridge from time to time, and maize and nuts in different seasons. He would care for the dogs and watch that the chickens didn't stray too far. And sometimes they might catch the large silver-scaled sabalo which swam in the mountain streams.

Baiya worried little about any inconveniences he would have to endure and even when Felisario puffed on his tobacco and filled the small thatched house with heavy plumes of smoke, he took it all in his stride. And there came a day when Felisario told his young friend that they would journey deep within the forest and there they would come to a place where the sacred vine grew tall and plentiful, twining itself high into the branches of the other trees in the jungle. There they would cut the vine, and give thanks to the spirits and bring the stalks back to their house. Then they would mash the stalks into a pulp and drink the sacred potion as the gods had done before them. New worlds would then open before them and Baiya would walk upon the path of the spirits, and see with a healer's eyes.

Early in the morning, as a blue-green mist still lingered in the trees, the two men headed off toward the north, carrying with them bows and lances, a bamboo knife and machete, and a good supply of arrows. Felisario also had with him a special bag to carry sections of the sacred vine.

For a while the path beneath the canopy was clear and open, the track lined with mosses, ferns and small white and yellow flowers. From time to time Felisario would kneel upon the ground to examine the footprints of the tapirs, wild pigs and other animals which sometimes crossed the track. Many had left behind their distinctive marks and odors, and in this way Felisario was able to learn the movements of the forest creatures that had recently passed this way.

Further along Felisario showed Baiya the distinctive trees which grew within the forest—the caimito with its succulent fruits, the giant lupuna which was home to different spirits, and the tall cauchero, or rubber tree, with its smooth grey bark. And from time to time they would hear the bustling howler monkeys in the branches above them, and pause to listen to the restless squawking of the red and blue macaws.

Soon the undergrowth became more tangled and the tracking much harder. Thorns scratched savagely against Baiya's legs, drawing blood, but fortunately Felisario knew which plants and leaves to rub upon his skin to ease the pain. Nevertheless, as they ventured still farther in the depths of the forest, Felisario became ever more cautious about the other creatures that lived there, for he knew that the smell of blood might draw a jaguar to their track and that poisonous vipers would also be harder to detect—their olive skins merging with the mossy bark of the trees. And so the two men moved carefully through the forest, ever watchful, ever alert to the creatures and unseen forces which surrounded them on their journey.

Finally they arrived at a clearing where Felisario often came when he was alone in the forest. Here he had built a small palm-thatch shelter, with a hammock draped above the ground and lashed with tight strips of bark. The sacred vine itself was just a short distance away through the trees, and the forest stream nearby would allow them to bathe and soothe their cuts.

After they had rested in the stream, Felisario told Baiya it was now time to cut the vine. They would place the stalks in the special bag which Felisario had brought with him, and they would then return home by nightfall to prepare the sacred potion.

Now as the two men walked toward the vine Felisario began to sing softly to himself, and he was singing the song which the Star-people sang when they first brought yajé to the peoples of the earth—a song which spoke of healing, and the power of the spirits. Then, as they stood before the vine, Felisario explained which parts would be cut. Using his machete he cut sections of the vine-stalk into small pieces and placed them carefully in his bag, giving thanks to the spirits for the blessings they had bestowed.

And now they knew they should return home as swiftly as possible, for this was the custom once the vine had been cut. And so the two men headed back through the forest, moving rapidly through the tangled undergrowth to the more open track ahead.

Even then a surprise awaited them, for as they drew closer to the open ground there was a scuffling in the bushes—and Felisario froze immediately in his tracks. But as he drew the leaves cautiously aside he could see that this was not a jaguar that stalked them but a small grey partridge fossicking in the earth.

With a quick thrust of his lance Felisario captured his prey, striking it through the breast. And for this, too, he gave thanks. The flesh from this creature would soon nourish their bodies, just as the juice from the sacred vine would later feed their souls.

Back at his house Felisario produced a large ceramic pot which was used only for drinking yajé. Decorated with yellow, white and red motifs, the pot was hung from the rafters when not in use, and Felisario took special care to see that it was always clean and well protected. "This helps us celebrate the spirits," he said with a broad smile on his face. "When we drink from this vessel we are joined to the Goddess, and she opens us to the path of vision."

But first they would have to crush the vine stalks into a mash, mixing the extracts with water and then passing the liquid through a small sieve. This they did outside the house in the fading light of day, simmering the brew over a low fire. And then, as evening fell, Felisario poured the liquid from the vine into the ceramic pot and brought it inside.

As they took their places on the palm matting in the center of the room, Felisario lit a small torch which sent shadows dancing across the palm-thatch roofing above their heads. Then he began to hum and shake his rattles, signaling to the spirits that the visionary encounters were about to begin.

Now he passed the pot across to Baiya and gestured for him to drink. And after Baiya had drunk from the vessel he too imbibed the milky fluid and then placed the pot on the floor, midway between them. "Most people know only one world," whispered Felisario to his young friend. "But the shaman must learn to leave his body and journey to other places with the spirits."

Felisario now placed his rattles beside him on the matting and added, "Now we will see what the Yajé Mother has in store for us."

For a short time Baiya could sense no change, but then the colors in the room became more vivid and intense, and soon he was watching Felisario through a haze of glowing amber light. And then it seemed that the pole uprights in the room had become large toucan feathers, and he was sitting on a bed of soft feather down. He himself had become a brightly colored bird—for his chest was now resplendent with red and yellow feathers and his arms had transformed into powerful, arching wings. And now he was flying in spirit beyond the forest clearing, beyond the crown of the tallest jungle trees—toward a mighty lupuna whose branches reached far up into the dark night sky.

As he flew closer to the lupuna he could see that the giant tree was alive with spirit-creatures—that little spheres of light had settled upon each of the branches like drops of crystal dew, and that within each of these spheres were strange animals and beings which he had never seen before. Now he was flying still higher through the branches of the tree, still higher until at last he reached its peak. And now he was soaring beyond the tree into the night sky, embracing each of the glistening stars in turn, and traveling ever more swiftly toward a vibrant silver light.

Baiya knew now that he had come to the realm of the Star-people, that his soul had been lifted up into the highest heavens. And from within the silver radiance which now enshrouded him, a tall and noble woman was gliding toward him, and her long and sinewy limbs were like the sacred vine itself. Her eyes were like the delicate pink flowers which grew upon its stem, and her long flowing hair was crowned with silver light. And he saw that she was naked to the waist.

Now she took him in her arms, and nestled him as if he were a new-born baby, and held his face before her large breasts so he could be nourished by her milk. And as Baiya drank in her beauty, drank in her sacred and wondrous mystery, he became one with the Goddess— one with a Goddess who had given birth to all the beings and creatures on this earth.

Then the Yajé Mother asked Baiya why he had come to visit her, and the purpose of his quest. And in asking this she knew his likely answer, for Baiya had long sought to journey among the spirits, to gain magic and healing powers, and to serve his people as a shaman.

But first, the Yajé Mother told him, he would have to face the all-conquering fear of death. And suddenly the silver radiance had gone, and the sky became intensely dark, and Baiya felt entwined by threatening, writhing snakes. These now encircled his entire body, coiling around his legs and arms, sliding through his hair and through the sockets of his eyes. And Baiya felt sure that he was now about to die, certain in the deepest corners of his soul that he had been forsaken by the Mother of the Earth.

And yet, just as he was about to surrender to their power, the coiled snakes fell away from his body and lay in passive formation around his feet. Then it seemed that they had joined together to become a single snake, a giant anaconda, and he was climbing upon its back as if riding on a horse. And now the snake was escorting him through the highest and most sacred heavens—realms far beyond the earth—and he was journeying once more among the stars, among the spirits of the sky where the Ancient Ones, the Star-people, had first made their home.

But gradually these visions passed from view, dissolving in a soft haze of light. And Baiya returned once more to the familiar world of life within the

forest, and his home within the clearing—to the
house with the palm-thatch roof, and the ceramic yajé
pot, and the matting upon the floor. And Felisario was
sitting across from him, watching him intently with a
broad smile on his face.

Already he had questions he wanted to ask.

"Did you see the Yajé Mother?" asked Felisario,
"and did you journey to the land of the Star-
people?"

Baiya nodded his head in agreement as Felisario
persisted with his questions.

"And how did you fly into the sky?" he asked.
"Did a spirit take you there?"

Baiya now told Felisario about his frightening
encounter with the coiled snakes, how he felt certain
that death had come to take his soul, and how he was
sure that his end had come. But then the snakes had
lain passively around his feet and had transformed into
a giant anaconda. And he had then mounted upon this
snake and ridden through the sky.

For a time Felisario remained silent as he reflected on these things, but then he rubbed his hands

together and nodded his head approvingly, quietly pleased that his young apprentice had ventured so powerfully within the world of gods and spirits.

"It is good that you saw all these things," he said finally. "It is good that you went to all these places and saw all these things, for you have journeyed to the home of the Ancient Ones and you have gained your first ally—and the anaconda is a powerful helper. Now the snake-spirit will be with you when you work as a healer."

All of these things Baiya remembered as he stood in silence beside the stream at the edge of the forest. All of these memories came flooding back to him as he listened to the welcome croaking of the frogs and toads, and to the gentle lapping of the water as it flowed across the stones.

But these events had taken place long ago, when he was still a young man, when he had ventured for the first time into the world of spirits and to the realm of the Yajé Mother. All of this was now many seasons past. And Baiya remembered too, with great sadness, that Felisario himself was no longer in the world of the living, that he had been swept away in the rapids above Xini Falls—in a tragic hunting accident much lamented by the people. Deep sorrow had been felt in the forest at that time, with the passing of a great and respected shaman.

It had long since fallen to Baiya to take the place of Felisario, and to continue on his path. And so Baiya was now known among his people as a healer who could suck out the evil spirits which captured human souls and which brought great and lasting sickness. Baiya was now well traveled upon the path of yajé and through this sacred plant new worlds had been opened to him. He was skilled in facing evil spirits and driving away their bewitching spells. And like Felisario, he too could see the sacred signs written in particles of light within the human soul, and he knew when sorcery had left its mark—for these sacred signs would then be scattered and broken, and must be made right again.

With the passing of Felisario, Baiya had returned once more to the master shaman's house, but this time he had set it ablaze, burning it to the ground. He had done this to free Felisario's soul, to ensure that he would not linger among the living but would instead wander off deep within the forest, and would then make his final journey back to the Star-people and to the home of the Yajé Mother in the sky. And Baiya no longer journeyed to Felisario's sacred vine but had now found another, and this vine too had similarly entwined itself within the tallest branches of the other trees.

Baiya and his family had built a large palm-thatch house on high land near a fresh mountain stream— and here they had planted crops of maize, nuts and sweet manioc, and also bananas and plantains, which they would roast on steaming coals. Baiya's sister Mira and his young wife Ruatay were with him now, and Mira's husband Forako, and his elderly mother Yopira—since the passing of his father. Now it was the turn of Baiya's son, Kavanti, to attend to the crops and dogs and chickens, and maintain the weed-infested gardens. And sometimes word would come from his brother Maleiwa, who lived far away in Iquitos, on the banks of the Amazon.

When he was still a young man, Maleiwa had gone to work in the rubber tree camps—for here he thought he would make his fortune. But the bosses had turned against him, and had called him a cholo, and looked down upon him as neither a city-worker nor a true Indian. Now he worked on the ferries which plied their way across the murky waters upstream from Iquitos, calling at different villages along the banks of the river. And his wife Katalina had taken work as a kitchen-hand with a family in the city.

After a season of heavy rains that from time to time swept the forest highlands, Mira and her husband Forako came down out of the mountains to journey to Iquitos. And finally, after traveling a great distance along the river, they came at last to the floating wooden houses and balsa rafts of Belén, where the poorest people lived. Then, further along, they arrived at Iquitos—with its large ships and ferries, and its paved streets and tiled buildings. Here they planned to stay for a time with Maleiwa and Katalina and their two young children, in a small brick house on the outskirts of the city.

But in the evenings, as Maleiwa sat with his family around the small wooden table—the kitchen lamp casting long gloomy shadows across the pale, flaking walls—Mira and Forako could see that a deep sadness had come into him, and they thought, perhaps, that his spirit had been lost amidst the sprawling streets of the unfamiliar city. Forako, meanwhile, was still full of memories of the forest and the mountains. He told Maleiwa about the long-house in the clearing and how the men would gather there from time to time, with their rattles and painted faces and toucan feather headbands. How great myths and stories would be shared, and sacred songs sung. And how each of the men would drink in turn from a sacred gourd—drink the potion which would open their hearts to the path of vision and to the world of spirits.

Forako could see then that Maleiwa felt a deep hunger for the ways of the past, a longing for the forest and the mountains. But now he was trapped here in the city and his soul was torn between different ways of living. And Maleiwa was like a frightened insect caught in the netting of a hunter-spider's web.

Maleiwa spoke then of working on the river, and how the river itself was alive with evil spirits. Sometimes these spirits would come into his dreams and he would awaken in the night—and at those times he would call out in panic for Katalina. And there was one spirit above all others which caused the greatest torment—a strange and powerful creature which lived deep within the river.

This spirit was Yacuruna, a fierce water-serpent that could make whirlpools rise up without warning. When these whirlpools came, boats would capsize and Yacuruna would drag its victims to the bottom of the river. At other times Yacuruna would rise up into the clouds and cause torrential rain to fall upon the land, and floods would then engulf the city, and people would be swept away to their deaths. And now Yacuruna was coming to taunt Maleiwa in the night, and he could hear the serpent writhing in the darkness, and smell its dank odor as it drew ever closer. Maleiwa feared that soon his soul would be snatched away by spirits of the darkness and he would be taken to the bottom of the river—and there his soul would be lost forever.

When Mira and Forako heard Maleiwa speak of these things they knew that dark times had come upon their brother and they must bring him back with them to Baiya, so that healing magic could be brought into his heart, and the evil spirits banished from his soul. And so, after talking in earnest with Katalina, and reassuring her that they would help make Maleiwa well again, Mira and Forako brought Maleiwa back to the mountains and the forest—back to his family and his people.

Two days later, while Maleiwa was still resting and as mist lingered in the tallest forest trees, Baiya and Forako headed off into the jungle, carrying with them bows and lances, a bamboo knife and machete, and a good supply of arrows. Now it was Baiya who brought the special bag to carry pieces of the sacred vine. And from time to time he would kneel upon the ground to examine the footprints of the wild animals which sometimes crossed the track.

Soon, after traveling south below Xini Falls, they came to the area of the forest where Baiya had found the tall yajé vine. It was fine and healthy, its highest sections bursting with clusters of small pink flowers. And now it was Baiya who sang the special spirit-songs in honor of the Star-people and the Yajé Mother, and it was he who cut sections of the vine-stalk and placed them in the bag. Then, after this was done, he and Forako headed back swiftly to the family long-house, so that they could mash the stalks, and mix the pulp with water, and pour the juice through a small sieve. And Kavanti had already prepared a small log fire, so the brew could simmer over a low heat.

Then, as dusk fell upon the forest and the chirpings of the night birds and the insects began to sound across the clearing, it was time to rouse Maleiwa from his rest and bring him to the center of the room where the sacred pot of yajé had been placed. And as Baiya and Forako poured the juice into a gourd, Mira and Ruatay sang healing songs of welcome—for they were pleased that Maleiwa had come to stay with them once more. In a corner of the long-house Yopira sat in silence upon her bed of matted palm leaves. She too was pleased her son was with them, and she offered prayers to the Ancient Ones, hoping that these evil spirits would soon be banished from his soul.

Now Baiya passed the gourd to Maleiwa and asked him to drink the sacred potion. And then Forako drank, and finally Baiya himself. Then, after a short time, they knew that the Ancient Ones and spirits had come among them in the long-house, for they began to shake and tremble deep within their souls, and a shimmering haze filled the long-house. And then a dazzling array of colors came down around them, and they swam within these colors as if in a glistening mountain stream.

And then Baiya looked deep within the luminous flickerings of Maleiwa's spirit-body, and he could see that the glistening particles of light which had been placed there by the gods were now scattered and broken. And evil spirits had come to haunt his soul.

So Baiya placed his lips upon Maleiwa's chest and began to suck with all his strength, drawing the evil spirits out of his brother's body so that they could be spat away and cast into the depths of the forest. And at the same time he was singing the sacred healing songs which had been given to his people, and he was pouring particles of light into Maleiwa's tortured soul, as if filling an empty vessel. Then for a time his brother's body became a place of torment, for the evil spirits were angry and they were fighting against these sacred powers of healing, and they did not choose to leave. Maleiwa tossed and turned through all of this, and his arms were flailing wildly in the air, but Baiya was there beside him. Finally, with the coming of the dawn, the evil spirits departed and the battle was won. Then Baiya shook his seed-pod rattles and chanted an ancient healing song, and Mira and Ruatay put their arms around their brother—to soothe and comfort him.

And when Baiya looked deep within Maleiwa's spirit-body he could see now that the glistening particles of light had come together and were written in his soul as the gods had chosen, and the way had been made right for Maleiwa once again. Then a gourd of manioc beer was passed around, and as Maleiwa drank from it he could feel his strength return and a new sense of well-being filled his soul.

Soon afterward, Baiya awoke early one morning and went to stand in silence beside the mountain stream. And once again he was comforted by the gentle lapping of the water as it flowed across the stones.

But he could feel also that a new sense of urgency had arisen within the forest, for his healing spirits were calling him, and they were telling him that all was not well with the Yajé Mother—that the spirit of the earth was falling out of balance and that the gifts and blessings of the gods were being torn and fragmented deep within its heart. And Baiya knew that a new calling would soon present itself, and the Ancient Ones would ask that he should join them on a quest—though he knew not what it was.

Later that evening Baiya summoned the senior men for a gathering in the long-house. And as night came down upon the forest, Baiya made his way across the clearing to the rocky track which led up to the meeting place. Away in the distance he could hear his dogs barking and the sound of chickens scratching in the earth. And within the depths of the forest the never-ending chirping of the night birds and the insects would continue until dawn.

Once again his face and arms were freshly painted with the special markings that were sacred to his people, and he had brought with him his rattles and his feather headband. And as he passed by the corn field and the cleared land beside the forest he could see that Forako and Maleiwa had come on ahead of him, and the other men were now arriving too. A torch had been lit inside the long-house and a small patch of reddish light shone forth from the entrance, blending with the intense darkness of the night.

Already some of the men had taken their places upon the small wooden stools around the hearth. And each of the men wore a headband of brightly colored toucan feathers and their olive-brown skins were glistening with vivid lines and motifs. Once again Setuma had brought the sacred jug of yajé, and he was wearing decorative seed rattles upon his elbows and his ankles. And Waka was playing upon his flute.

As Baiya entered the long-house the other men turned to greet him, for on this special evening it would again fall to him to pass the sacred bowls of yajé from person to person, among those who had gathered there.

Now Setuma placed the pot of yajé in the center of the room, where the torch had been lit, and soon it was time for Baiya to pass the potion around. After stirring the liquid with a wooden stick, Baiya poured it into two gourd vessels and then, as these were passed from one man to the next, Waka began to play once more upon his flute while Forako and Maleiwa hummed and sang.

Soon the spirits of the yajé had come among them, for the men began to shake and tremble and they were caught up in a swirling torrent which threatened to subsume them, like an omen from the gods. And once again the wooden posts within the long-house became richly jeweled snakes that writhed and twisted and climbed up into the rafters. And a shrill wailing of spirit-voices chorused through the air.

Now as Baiya sat with his friends amidst the dazzling colors of the long-house, his soul began to lift up out of his body like a crystal bird, and once again he was flying high into the dark night sky— toward the highest heavens above the earth. And again a haze of silver radiance enshrouded him as the tall and noble Yajé Mother came toward him, her eyes glistening like the delicate pink flowers which grew upon the vine, her long flowing hair crowned with silver light.

But now he could see that her eyes were filled with tears, and a deep sorrow possessed her heart. And the Yajé Mother told him that the world was yet again heading for a time of fierce storms and upheaval, and that the Ancient Ones were greatly angered by the ways of the people.

For in all lands upon the earth the people had turned their faces away from the Ancient Ones whose gift of life had been bestowed with loving intent, and the people no longer remembered the sacred teachings which had been given to them since earliest times. Now men's souls were havens for evil spirits, and even mothers and young ones overlooked the customs they had learned. And people could no longer place their bond of trust with one another, for the very song of life had vanished from their hearts.

But the Yajé Mother told Baiya that the world was not forsaken, that there would be a cleansing and a renewal, and a coming forth of a new world from the old. Trusted shamans and healers from each of the four directions would be summoned by the Ancient Ones to the very center of the earth. And here the Great Song of Life would rise up once again, and the great gods and spirits from the heavens and the earth would bestow their blessings upon the people of all lands—for this was the only way forward.

And the Great Spirit had called for a worthy and trusted messenger who would come forward from the West—one who could help restore the ancient ways of knowing. And it had been decreed that the Yajé Mother would bring this trusted messenger to a sacred place where all hunting tracks meet, and where all spirits are One Spirit. And he, Baiya, had been chosen to be present at the rebirth of the world.

Now she told him that they must journey together, through a secret entrance behind the thundering waters of Xini Falls. And once they had passed through this entrance, a path would then take them down into the lower world.

And so Baiya and the Yajé Mother passed through the secret entrance on a rock ledge behind Xini Falls, safe from the cascading waters, and made their way to a deep and sacred place far below the forest and the mountains.

And it was in this way that they came finally to the Great Lake of Spirit at the very center of the world—a lake which had always existed, even before the world had come into being. And this was the sacred sea from which All Things Come Forth.

Baiya and the Yajé Mother knew that they must now wait beside this lake until the appointed time, for they had heard that in other lands, too, the Ancient Ones had also gone in search of loyal and worthy messengers. That from each of the four directions—from North, South, East and West—shamans would be summoned as custodians of the Great Spirit, and they would journey to this sacred place.

But now, from the West, Baiya had come—as a trusted and worthy shaman. And he would serve as a witness to the healing of the earth.

CENTER

Then the noble and timeless Song of the Great Spirit could be heard across the waters, and it came like a beautiful, sacred chorus with the chiming of a thousand crystal bells—and the four shamans from North, South, East and West were welcomed to the sacred shores.

First, from the North, Enoyuk was called—and he took his place beside the edge of the Great Lake of Spirit, the eternal lake from which All Things Come Forth. And as he stood beside this lake, looking out into its infinite and mysterious depths, he saw that it was like a vast and awesome mirror which reached out in all directions, and that all things which happened in the world were written in its waters. He saw too that all the great stories and all the sacred songs of his people had come forth from this place, and that this too was the birthplace of the Ancient Ones—the gods and goddesses who watched over his people, and who had provided them with purpose, truth and meaning since the earliest times.

And as Enoyuk looked further within the mirror of its waters he could see Nuliajuk, Mistress of the Animals, in her home at the bottom of the ocean, and now Sila, Lord of the Air, had returned to his place of dominion upon the mountain peaks, where he caused strong winds to rise up and brought breath to all living things. And even beyond them, Enoyuk caught glimpses of the nameless Creator God who had first brought light to the dark world of Earth, and there he also saw Raven—who had been called to be his special helper. These things Enoyuk saw, and he knew then that his own soul had first come forth from the Great Lake of Spirit, and that all things and all beings had come forth from one place—an ancient, time-less place which had always existed, even before the creation of the world.

Now Kalu was called from the South to the edge of the Great Lake of Spirit, and as he looked forth into its shining waters he too could see that this was the first home of his sacred songs and Dreamings. For this was where the Crystal Father, timeless and revered Father of the Sky, had been born amidst the thunderclouds and lightning which had first burst upon the earth. And it was here too that the sacred Rainbow Serpent, Mother of all Living Creatures, had first found her place within the rocks and waterholes which had come into existence with the Dawn of Creation. And from these first rocks and waterholes had come the sacred song-tracks which meshed their way across the red earth, so that all custodians chosen by the people would know these secret stories, and would strive to honor and protect them from this time forth.

Then, from the East, it was the turn of Saimei to come to the edge of the Great Lake of Spirit. And as she cast her gaze within the crystal depths, she could see that this was the true home of the sacred kami-spirits and the Goddess of the Waters. For they too had first come from this eternal lake of spirit, and they had brought with them the gifts of life and hope and well-being. And they had then come among the people, and through the cycles of the seasons their healing powers and blessings had flowed down from Mount Ikuta to the valleys and the streams. And Saimei saw that this had always been so, even from the earliest times since the birth of all Creation.

Finally, from the West, Baiya stood beside the edge of the Great Lake of Spirit. And now, for him also, it was like a mirror to the soul. And as he looked deep within the shining waters Baiya could see all the forests and mountains and waterfalls which had ever existed in the world, and the spirit-creatures which lived there in their midst. And there too he could see giant yajé vines growing in the forest, vines which extended so high that their highest tips reached up and touched the stars.

Then, within the depths of the Spirit Lake, Baiya could see the glistening torches of the Star-people as they brought the yajé down to Earth, and he watched as they showed the first Ancestors how to use this sacred plant for their magic and their healing. And he knew then that waters from the Spirit Lake had first nourished the sacred vine, and it was here that the Yajé Mother had been born. And even when she was still a little child her eyes had glistened like the delicate pink flowers which grew upon the vine, and even then her long flowing hair was crowned with silver light.

Then, when they had seen these things, the four shamans from North, South, East and West turned their gaze to the center of the Great Lake of Spirit. For now a glorious and wonderful song had arisen from deep within the infinite and mysterious waters. And it was even more beautiful, even more haunting than the sacred chorus and chiming crystal bells which had welcomed them before. And this was the Song of the Great Spirit.

The Song of the Great Spirit spoke first of the troubles and turbulence which had come upon the world, and how the sacred earth had been soiled and tarnished by the wrongdoings of the people. How many had turned away from the sacred teachings which had brought all peoples together, and which had been with them always. And how the gods and goddesses from all lands and places had poured their tears upon the earth when they had seen how far the people had fallen from the sacred ways of being.

But now the Song of the Great Spirit proclaimed that the world would be reborn, and new life would flow through its veins, coursing like a mighty torrent through the seas and streams and rivers, through the forests and deserts and snow-tipped mountains. And the blemishes and wrongdoings which had been wrought upon the earth would be undone, and the poisons which now choked the land and oceans would be cleansed and washed away.

And as they watched in awe beside the Great Lake of Spirit, the sky was filled with a dazzling golden light, and the heavens resounded with a sacred Song of Healing, whose majestic and uplifting melodies proclaimed the cleansing of the world. And the power from this song moved deep within the Earth, reaching now into every crack and crevice and into every flowing stream. Already it resounded within every living creature, and within every human heart. And a new blessing had come upon the Earth, and the gods and goddesses from all lands and peoples saw that it was good.

It seemed then that the world had come to both an end and a beginning, and the shamans from North, South, East and West knew that they had shared a sacred purpose—a quest which had brought them from the four corners of the Earth. And this was to keep pure the sacred ways of being, to honor all living creatures and to value the teachings which had been given to them by the Ancient Ones. For they knew now that even the greatest gods and goddesses had been born in the infinite waters, that they too had their home and birthplace within the Great Lake of Spirit. And that all things and all beings had come forth from one place—an ancient and timeless place which had always existed, even before the creation of the world.

About SKYLIGHT PATHS Publishing

SkyLight Paths Publishing is creating a place where people of different spiritual traditions come together for challenge and inspiration, a place where we can help each other understand the mystery that lies at the heart of our existence.

Through spirituality, our religious beliefs are increasingly becoming a part of our lives—rather than *apart* from our lives. While many of us may be more interested than ever in spiritual growth, we may be less firmly planted in traditional religion. Yet, we do want to deepen our relationship to the sacred, to learn from our own as well as from other faith traditions, and to practice in new ways.

SkyLight Paths sees both believers and seekers as a community that increasingly transcends traditional boundaries of religion and denomination—people wanting to learn from each other, *walking together, finding the way.*

We at SkyLight Paths take great care to produce beautiful books that present meaningful spiritual content in a form that reflects the art of making high quality books. Therefore, we want to acknowledge those who contributed to the production of this book.

PRODUCTION
Tim Holtz, Martha McKinney & Bridgett Taylor

EDITORIAL
Amanda Dupuis, Polly Short Mahoney,
Lauren Seidman & Emily Wichland

COVER DESIGN
Drena Fagen, New York, New York

PRINTING & BINDING
Versa Press, East Peoria, Illinois

Other Interesting Books—Spirituality

Lighting the Lamp of Wisdom: *A Week Inside a Yoga Ashram*
by *John Ittner;* Foreword by *Dr. David Frawley*

This insider's guide to Hindu spiritual life takes you into a typical week of retreat inside a yoga ashram to demystify the ashram experience and show you what to expect from your own visit. Includes a discussion of worship services, meditation and yoga classes, chanting and music, work practice, and more.

6 x 9, 224 pp, b/w photographs, Quality PB Original, ISBN 1-893361-52-7 **$15.95**; HC, ISBN 1-893361-37-3 **$24.95**

Waking Up: *A Week Inside a Zen Monastery*
by *Jack Maguire;* Foreword by *John Daido Loori, Roshi*

An essential guide to what it's like to spend a week inside a Zen Buddhist monastery.

6 x 9, 224 pp, b/w photographs, HC, ISBN 1-893361-13-6 **$21.95**

  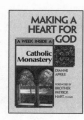 

Making a Heart for God: *A Week Inside a Catholic Monastery*
by *Dianne Aprile;* Foreword by *Brother Patrick Hart, OCSO*

This essential guide to experiencing life in a Catholic monastery takes us to the Abbey of Gethsemani—the Trappist monastery in Kentucky that was home to author Thomas Merton—to explore the details. "More balanced and informative than the popular *The Cloister Walk* by Kathleen Norris." —*Choice: Current Reviews for Academic Libraries*

6 x 9, 224 pp, b/w photographs, Quality PB, ISBN 1-893361-49-7 **$16.95**; HC, ISBN 1-893361-14-4 **$21.95**

Come and Sit: *A Week Inside Meditation Centers*
by *Marcia Z. Nelson;* Foreword by *Wayne Teasdale*

The insider's guide to meditation in a variety of different spiritual traditions. Traveling through Buddhist, Hindu, Christian, Jewish, and Sufi traditions, this essential guide takes the reader to different meditation centers to meet the teachers and students and learn about the practices, demystifying the meditation experience for people of all levels.

6 x 9, 224 pp, b/w photographs, Quality PB Original, ISBN 1-893361-35-7 **$16.95**

Or phone, fax, mail or e-mail to: SKYLIGHT PATHS Publishing
Sunset Farm Offices, Route 4 • P.O. Box 237 • Woodstock, Vermont 05091
Tel: (802) 457-4000 Fax: (802) 457-4004 www.skylightpaths.com
Credit card orders: (800) 962-4544 (9AM–5PM ET Monday–Friday)
Generous discounts on quantity orders. SATISFACTION GUARANTEED. Prices subject to change.

Spirituality

Earth, Water, Fire, and Air: *Essential Ways of Connecting to Spirit*
by *Cait Johnson*

Spiritual nourishment at its most basic—
the elemental approach to spirituality

You can't help but be drawn into the elemental approach to spirituality so gracefully detailed in this book. It identifies the four basic elements as humanity's first ways of knowing Spirit and reminds us of their value as keys to self-healing and re-connection. Offers a fascinating look at element-based symbols, traditions, and ceremonies, with creative activity suggestions for both individuals and groups. 6 x 9, 224 pp, Hardcover, ISBN 1-893361-65-9 **$19.95**

Praying with Our Hands: *Twenty-One Practices of Embodied Prayer from the World's Spiritual Traditions*
by *Jon M. Sweeney*; Photographs by *Jennifer J. Wilson*;
Foreword by *Mother Tessa Bielecki*; Afterword by *Taitetsu Unno, Ph.D.*

A spiritual guidebook for bringing prayer into our bodies.

This inspiring book of reflections and accompanying photographs shows us twenty-one simple ways of using our hands to speak to God, to enrich our devotion and ritual. All express the various approaches of the world's religious traditions to bringing the body into worship. Spiritual traditions represented include Anglican, Sufi, Zen, Roman Catholic, Yoga, Shaker, Hindu, Jewish, Pentecostal, Eastern Orthodox, and many others.
8 x 8, 96 pp, 22 duotone photographs, Quality PB Original, ISBN 1-893361-16-0 **$16.95**

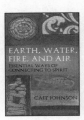   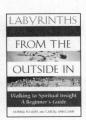

The Sacred Art of Listening
Forty Reflections for Cultivating a Spiritual Practice
by *Kay Lindahl*; Illustrations by *Amy Schnapper*

More than ever before, we need to embrace the skills and practice of listening. You will learn to: Speak clearly from your heart • Communicate with courage and compassion • Heighten your awareness for deep listening • Enhance your ability to listen to people with different belief systems. 8 x 8, 160 pp, Illus., Quality PB Original, ISBN 1-893361-44-6 **$16.95**

Labyrinths from the Outside In
Walking to Spiritual Insight—a Beginner's Guide
by *Donna Schaper* and *Carole Ann Camp*

The user-friendly, interfaith guide to making and using labyrinths—
for meditation, prayer, and celebration.

Labyrinth walking is a spiritual exercise *anyone* can do. This accessible guide unlocks the mysteries of the labyrinth for all of us, providing ideas for using the labyrinth walk for prayer, meditation, and celebrations to mark the most important moments in life. Includes instructions for making a labyrinth of your own and finding one in your area.
6 x 9, 208 pp, b/w illus. and photographs, Quality PB Original, ISBN 1-893361-18-7 **$16.95**